FOC
$4

D1451975

SMALL & CHIC INTERIORS

SMALL & CHIC INTERIORS

Manel Gutiérrez

WITHDRAWN

KÖNEMANN

© 2018 koenemann.com GmbH
www.koenemann.com

ÉDITIONS
PLACE DES
VICTOIRES

© 2018 Éditions Place des Victoires
6, rue du Mail – 75002 Paris,
pour la présente édition.
www.victoires.com
Dépôt légal : 3e trimestre 2018
ISBN : 978-2-8099-1605-8

booq
publishing

Editorial coordination: Claudia Martínez Alonso
Art direction: Mireia Casanovas Soley
Edition and texts: Manel Gutiérrez (@mgutico)
Texts: Aleix Ortuño Velilla
Layout: Sara Abril
Translations: Thinking Abroad

Printed in China by Shenzhen Hua Xin Colour-printing & Platemaking Co., Ltd

ISBN 978-3-7419-2083-7

INTERIOR DG

INT2architecture
www.int2architecture.ru
Moscow, Russia
150 sq ft (14 m²)
© INT2architecture

This project is INT2architecture's interpretation of a small bedroom suitable for a 14 year old. The main objective was to create a comfortable and elegant atmosphere in which the youngster could carry out her daily life. To achieve this, they freed up half the space by taking the items that would usually be stored there and locating them in the other half of the room.

Bei diesem Projekt handelt es sich um die Interpretation eines kleinen Zimmer für ein 14-jähriges Mädchen des Studios INT2architecture. Das Hauptziel bestand darin, dem Mädchen eine bequeme und elegante Atmosphäre für das tägliche Leben zu bieten. Der Vorschlag zielt darauf ab, die eine Hälfte des Raums von den vielen Gegenständen zu befreien, die man in jedem Zimmer findet, und sie in der anderen Hälfte unterzubringen.

Ce projet est l'interprétation qu'INT2architecture a faite pour une petite chambre destinée à une jeune fille de 14 ans. Le but principal est que la vie quotidienne de celle-ci se déroule dans un cadre confortable et élégant. C'est pourquoi la moitié de l'espace se retrouve dégagée des différents objets qui encombrent toute pièce. Ceux-ci sont renvoyés vers l'autre moitié.

Este proyecto es la interpretación que INT2architecture hace de una pequeña habitación para una joven de 14 años. El objetivo principal es que la vida cotidiana de la joven transcurra en un ambiente cómodo y elegante. Para ello, la propuesta libera la mitad del espacio de los diferentes objetos independientes que suelen poblar cualquier estancia, albergándolos en la otra mitad.

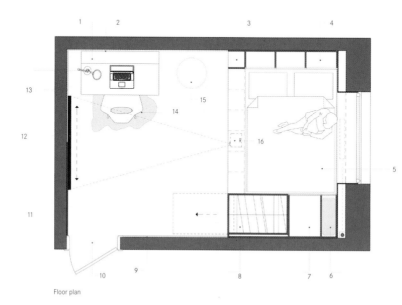

Floor plan

1. Desk
2. Pictures
3. Bookshelves
4. Shelves
5. Mattress
6. Shelf for back
   pillows of the sofa
7. Compartment for
   clothes
8. Wardrobe
9. Hooks
10. Door
11. Mirror
12. Sliding screen
13. Blackboard
14. Organic chair
15. Basket for pillows
16. Projector

The multifunctional surface is a sliding panel which, depending on its position, opens a white board or a mirror. When positioned in the centre it opens the projector screen.

Die multifunktionale Oberfläche ist ein Schiebepaneel, das in verschiedenen Positionen entweder eine Tafel, einen Spiegel oder in der Mitte die Leinwand für den Projektor freigibt.

La surface multifonctions est un panneau coulissant dont les positions révèlent un tableau noir, un miroir ou l'écran du projecteur (en position centrale).

La superficie multifuncional es un panel deslizante que, en diferentes posiciones, abre una pizarra, un espejo o, en la posición central, la pantalla del proyector.

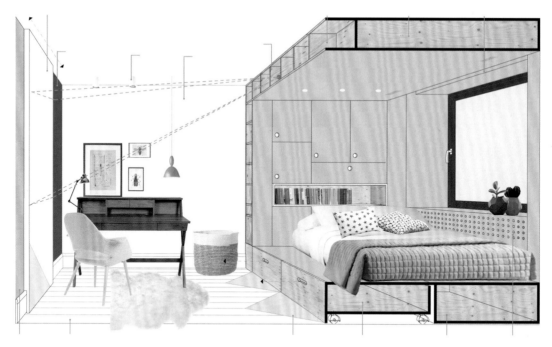

3D section

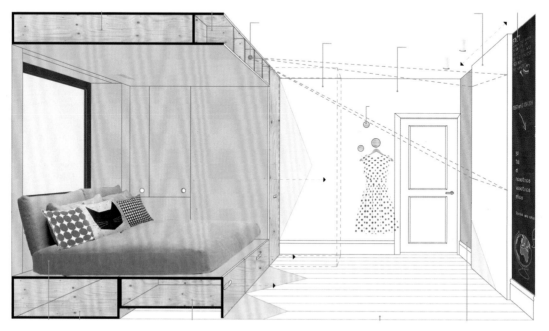

3D section

This multifunctional box houses a compact storage system, with wardrobe, drawers, shelves and even a sofa bed on which to sleep.

Der multifunktionale Würfel beinhaltet ein Ordnungssystem: Kleiderschrank, Schubladen und Regale, wie auch das Sofa-Bett zum Schlafen.

La boîte multifonctionnelle abrite un système de rangement compact : armoire, commode et étagères, ainsi que le canapé-lit destiné au repos.

La caja multifuncional alberga un sistema compacto de almacenamiento: armario, cajonera y estanterías, además del sofá cama donde dormir.

MINI STUDIO

Ajay Chopra / Echo: Design + Architecture
www.echoda.com
New York, NY, USA
215 sq ft (20 m^2)
© Javier Oddo Photography

When setting out to design a small space, one of the key objectives is to make it appear larger than it actually is. By installing custom-made floor-to-ceiling cabinets and including storage spaces beneath the bed, this objective is easily met and so too are many of the design aspects of this project addressed.

Eines der Hauptziele beim Umsetzen eines Designs in kleinen Räumen besteht darin, zu erreichen, dass diese größer wirken als sie sind, Der Einbau von Schranken, die vom Boden bis zur Decke reichen, und Lagerungsmöglichkeiten unter dem Bett tragen dazu bei, dieses Ziel aus der Entwurfsphase dieses Projekts zu erreichen

L'un des buts principaux lors de la conception d'espaces réduits est de réussir à les faire paraître plus grands qu'ils ne le sont vraiment. L'installation d'armoires sur mesure, en pleine hauteur, ainsi que d'espaces de rangement en dessous du lit permet sans aucun doute que cet objectif soit atteint. Il l'est largement dans le cas de ce projet.

Uno de los principales objetivos a la hora de abordar el diseño de espacios reducidos es conseguir que estos parezcan más amplios de lo que en realidad son. La instalación de armarios a medida, que ocupan toda la altura del apartamento, y de espacios de almacenamientos debajo de la cama permiten, sin duda, que el objetivo se cumpla, y con creces, en el diseño de este proyecto.

Each element of this apartment has a dual purpose, for example the door and cupboard panels can be reversed in order to double up as a table.

Jedes Element der Wohnung erfüllt einen zweifachen Zweck: Die Türpaneele oder das Mobiliar können gedreht werden und verwandeln sich dann in kleine Theken.

Chaque élément de l'appartement a une double fonction : en retournant les panneaux des portes ou les meubles, ceux-ci peuvent se transformer en comptoirs.

Cada elemento del apartamento tiene un doble propósito: los paneles de las puertas o el mobiliario, al darles la vuelta, pueden transformarse en mostradores.

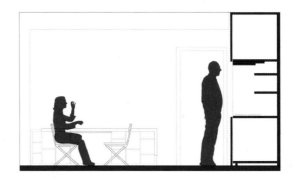

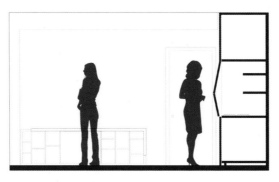

Sections of the kitchen

Floor plan

1. Bedroom
2. Bathroom
3. Kitchen
4. Storage room
5. Living room/Dining room

The wall of white panels is revealed as a single kitchen only when necessary. The frosted glass sliding door provides both privacy and light.

Die Wand aus weißen Paneelen entpuppt sich nur dann als Küche, wenn es nötig ist. Die verspiegelte Glastür kann man hin und herschieben: Sie verleiht dem Raum eine gewisse Privatsphäre, lässt aber auch Licht hindurch.

Le mur aux panneaux blancs dévoile la cuisine lorsqu'il y en a besoin. La porte coulissante en verre poli offre de l'intimité et de la lumière à la fois.

La pared de paneles blancos se revela como una cocina solo cuando es necesario. La puerta de cristal esmerilado deslizante proporciona a la vez privacidad y luz.

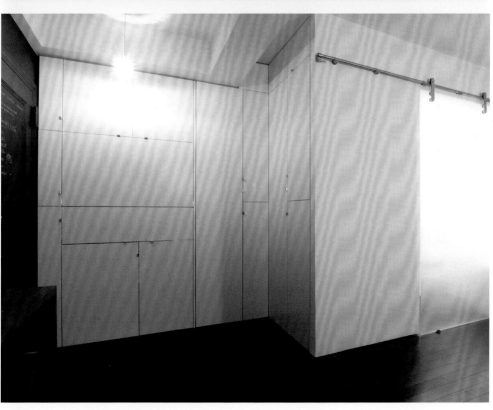

THE PURPLE ROSE OF CAIRO

Architecture Architecture
www.archarch.com.au
Melbourne, Australia
258 sq ft (24 m^2)
© Tom Ross of Brilliant Creek

The Cairo Apartments are a symbol of Melbourne architecture, a collection of tiny dwellings that, even in 1936, were a firm reference to minimalism. Architecture Architecture took on the task of fitting out one of the apartments and making it more flexible. When dealing with such a small space, a firm hand is vital. The slightest hesitation can ruin the effect.

Die Cairo Apartments sind ein architektonisches Wahrzeichen Melbournes. Es handelt sich um kleine Wohnungen, die bereits in 1936 ein minimalistischer Bezugspunkt waren. Architecture Architecture haben versucht, eine der Wohnung auszustatten und flexibler zu gestalten. In einem kleinen Raum so umfassend einzugreifen bedeutet behutsam, aber bestimmt zu sein: Die kleinste Unschlüssigkeit zerstört den erreichten Eindruck.

Les appartements du Caire sont un emblème de l'architecture de Melbourne, des logements minuscules qui étaient déjà une référence minimaliste en 1936. Architecture Architecture a entrepris la tâche d'équiper et de rendre l'un des appartements plus flexible. En intervenant dans un espace si petit, un doigté précis est vital, car toute hésitation peut anéantir les sensations créées.

Los Apartamentos Cairo son un emblema de la arquitectura de Melbourne, unas minúsculas viviendas que, ya en 1936, eran todo un referente minimalista. Architecture Architecture emprendió la tarea de equipar y hacer más flexible uno de los apartamentos. Al intervenir en un espacio tan pequeño, el pulso firme es vital: cualquier vacilación puede romper las sensaciones logradas.

A simple curtain and folding bed provide all the necessary combinations: a bedroom, a dining room, a study, a meeting place...

Ein einfacher Vorhang und ein Faltbett sorgen für alle möglichen Kombinationen: Schlafzimmer, Esszimmer, Studio, Treffpunkt...

Un simple rideau et un lit escamotable offrent toutes les combinaisons nécessaires : une chambre, une salle à manger, un atelier, une salle de réunions...

Una simple cortina y una cama plegable ofrecen todas las combinaciones necesarias: un dormitorio, un comedor, un estudio, un lugar de reunión...

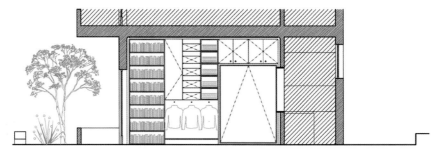

Section

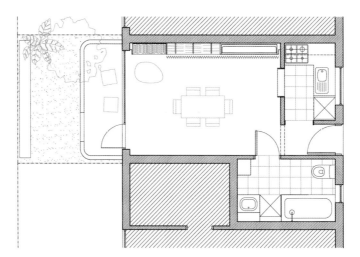

Floor plan dining mode

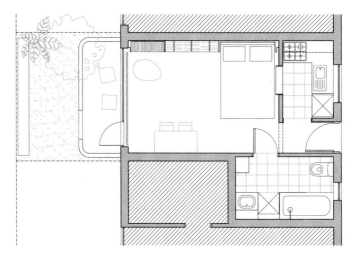

Floor plan bedroom mode

All the apartments have access to a communal garden. By opening up a service window one is able to enjoy it from the kitchen.

Alle Wohnungen gehen auf einen gemeinsamen Garten hinaus. Die Öffnung eines der Fenster ermöglicht es von der Küche aus, diesen Garten zu genießen.

Tous les appartements ont accès à un jardin communautaire. On en profite depuis la cuisine, par l'ouverture d'une fenêtre de service.

Todos los apartamentos tienen acceso a un jardín comunitario. La obertura de una ventana de servicio le permite a la cocina disfrutar de él.

FLAT 75018-1

Labro and Davis
www.labrodavis.com
Paris, France
322 sq ft (30m^2)
© Labro & Davis

This renovated Parisian studio is reminiscent of a Russian doll, with one functional space nestled within another in order to accommodate an entire house within a miniscule space. But it is not just the efficient organisation of the space that provides life to this home. Air flows through the building from end to end, as does the light. The two are indispensable in this design.

Dieser Umbau eines Pariser Studios wirkt wie eine russische Matroschka: In jedem funktionalen Raum befindet sich ein anderer funktionaler Raum, um dann zusammen eine komplette Wohnung auf kleinster Fläche zu bilden. Der Mensch lebt jedoch nicht nur von der effizienten Organisation des Wohnraums. Die Luft durchströmt die gesamte Wohnung ebenso wie das Licht. Eine unabdingbare Voraussetzung.

La restructuration de cet appartement parisien a quelque chose de l'âme d'une poupée russe ; chaque espace fonctionnel se niche au sein d'un autre, pour créer un appartement complet, sur une surface minuscule. L'homme ne vit pas que de l'organisation efficace de l'espace. L'air et la lumière le traversent de part et d'autre. Une condition indispensable.

Esta remodelación de un estudio parisino tiene alma de muñeca rusa: anida cada espacio funcional dentro de otro espacio funcional para dar cabida a un apartamento completo en una superficie minúscula. Pero no solo de la organización eficiente del espacio vive el hombre. El aire atraviesa la casa de parte a parte, y lo mismo hace la luz. Son requerimiento indispensable.

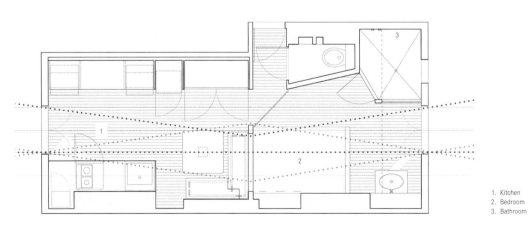

Floor plan

1. Kitchen
2. Bedroom
3. Bathroom

When one cannot look too far without the eye meeting a wall, the eye simply shuns the horizon beyond the window. Tiny houses depend on this.

Wenn man nicht weiter in die Ferne blicken kann, da eine Mauer einem die Sicht versperrt, wird das Auge von den großen Fenstern und dem Horizont angezogen. Die kleinsten Häuser hängen davon ab.

Quand on ne peut voir trop loin sans se cogner à un mur, le regard fuit vers l'horizon, au-delà de la fenêtre. Les maisons minuscules dépendent de celui-ci.

Cuando uno no puede mirar demasiado lejos antes de darse de bruces con una pared, los ojos le huyen al horizonte tras la ventana. Las casas minúsculas dependen de él.

LA MANSARDA DI STELLA

Spazio 14 10 team: Stella Passerini, Giulia Peruzzi
www.spazio1410.com
Rome, Italy
320 sq ft (30 m²)
© Spazio 14 10: Stella Passerini

This uncompromising commitment to chic uses recycled materials in order to achieve its aims. "We want to bring interior design to the people" say architects Spazio 14 10. Indeed, Stella represents the people, and her loft seems to demonstrate that design is within the reach of many. It all began with just 355 sq ft and a limited budget. The result is extraordinary.

Dieser hohe Einsatz für den ästhetischen Schick bedient sich recycelter Materialien, um es bis auf die Spitze zu treiben. „Wir wollten den Leuten das Innendesign näher bringen", sagt das Team von Spazo 14 10. Stella ist ganz offensichtlich ,die Leute' und ihre Dachkammer beweist, dass eine solche Dekoration in Reichweite vieler Personen ist. Die Voraussetzungen sind beschränkt und nur 33 m² groß: das Resultat verwirrt.

Ce pari décidé sur l'esthétique chic se sert de matériaux recyclés pour atteindre ses objectifs. « Nous voulons rendre l'architecture d'intérieur accessible aux gens », dit l'agence Spazio 14 10. Ainsi à l'exemple de Stella : ses combles semblent prouver qu'une telle décoration est à la portée de beaucoup. Avec un budget limité et 33 m², le résultat est troublant.

Esta apuesta a ultranza por la estética chic se sirve de los materiales reciclados para alcanzar su cima. "Queremos acercar el diseño de interiores a la gente", dicen desde Spazio 14 10. Stella es gente, por supuesto, y su ático parece demostrar que una decoración así está al alcance de muchos. Se partió de un presupuesto limitado y 33 metros cuadrados: el resultado apabulla.

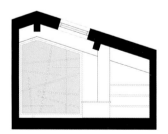

Cross section

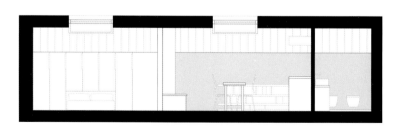

Longitudinal section

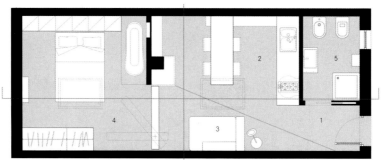

Floor plan

1. Entrance
2. Kitchen/Dinning room
3. Living room
4. Bedroom
5. Bathroom

This renovated antique bathroom wasn't in the budget so they slotted it into the bedroom. With the bed is next to it, it is the epitome of chic.

Diese alte und umgebaute Badewanne passt nicht nur größenmäßig hinein, sondern wurde noch in das Zimmer integriert. Das Bett ist nebenan. Der Inbegriff des Schicks.

Cette ancienne baignoire rénovée est rentrée non seulement dans le budget, mais aussi dans la pièce. Le lit est à côté, un épitomé du chic.

Esta antigua bañera remodelada no solo encajó dentro del presupuesto, sino que hicieron encajarla dentro de la habitación. La cama está al lado. Epítome de lo chic.

SHERBROOKE HOUSE

Russian for Fish
www.russianforfish.com
London, UK
376 sq ft (35 m^2)
© Peter Landers

Originally this space was a duplex with a very cramped feel to the ground floor layout and a gloomy and restrictive kitchen space. Russian for Fish's renovation project involved opening up the floor into a large kitchen-diner, flooded with natural light and benefitting from the beautiful south-facing garden.

Bei dem ursprünglichen Raum handelte es sich um eine Maisonette-Wohnung, in deren Untergeschoss die Aufteilung der Zimmer eine bedrückende Atmosphäre hervorrief und die Küchenzeile war dunkel und eng. Die Renovierung durch Russian for Fish sorgte dafür, dass der Raum nun eine große Koch-Essecke beinhaltet, in der alles vom Licht durchflutet ist und man den schönen Blick auf den gen Süden liegenden Garten auch genießen kann.

L'espace d'origine était un duplex dont la distribution des pièces au niveau inférieur créait une forte sensation d'étouffement, avec une cuisine sombre et étroite. La rénovation par Russian for Fish décloisonne ce niveau en une cuisine/salle à manger, où la lumière inonde tout l'espace et où l'on peut profiter des belles vues sur le jardin orienté sud.

El espacio original era un dúplex con una planta baja donde la distribución de las estancias producía una acusada sensación de agobio, y la cocina era un espacio oscuro y restrictivo. La renovación de Russian for Fish abre la planta en una gran área de cocina-comedor, donde la luz inunda todo el espacio y se aprovechan las bellas vistas al jardín, orientado al sur.

The kitchen furniture is designed to provide maximum storage space and create a feeling of subtle separation from the entrance hall.

Die Küchenmöbel wurden mit dem Ziel entworfen, den größtmöglichen Lagerraum und eine subtile Abtrennung mit dem Vestibül des Eingangsbereichs zu schaffen.

Les meubles de cuisine sont conçus dans le but de permettre un rangement maximum et de garantir une séparation subtile d'avec le hall d'entrée.

Los muebles de cocina está diseñados con el fin de permitir el máximo almacenamiento y proporcionar una sutil separación con el vestíbulo de la entrada.

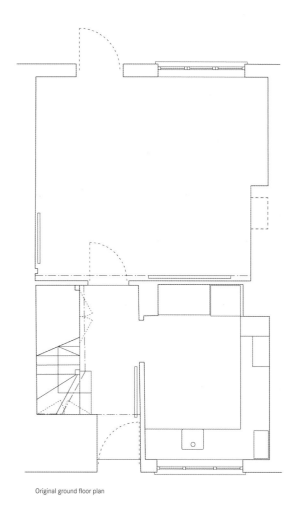

Original ground floor plan

Project ground floor plan

1.   Reception
2.   Hall
3.   Kitchen

HB6B – ONE HOME

Karin Matz
www.karinmatz.se
Stockholm, Sweden
387 sq ft (36 m^2)
© Karin Matz

All the planning in the world could not have achieved the rickety, atypical style that permeates this ultramodern apartment renovation. The secret is that only a part of it has been remodelled. It remains what is was, a flat that was used to store furniture for 30 years, with bare walls and a bathroom that was overrun with rats. We should mention that the bathroom *has* been updated.

Mit keinem Vorsatz der Welt hätte man dieses klapprige und unübliche Aussehen erschaffen können, das diese modernistische Renovierung einer Wohnung aufweist. Das Geheimnis: Ein Teil wurde kaum renoviert. Er ist einfach das, was er schon immer war. Eine Wohnung, in der 30 Jahre lang Möbel aufbewahrt wurden, die Wände waren nicht tapeziert und das Bad war in der Hand der Ratten. An dieser Stelle sei erwähnt: Das Bad wurde *doch* renoviert.

Même avec toute la volonté du monde, on n'aurait pu rendre l'aspect délabré et désuet de cette restructuration super-moderne. Le secret est qu'une partie seulement a été rénovée. Cet appartement usé continue à être ce qu'il était, un garde-meubles pendant 30 ans, aux murs dénudés et avec une salle de bains à la merci des rats. Le bain a vraiment été rénové, il faut le dire.

Ni toda la premeditación del mundo hubiera logrado el aspecto desvencijado y desusado que luce esta modernísima remodelación de un apartamento. El secreto: una parte apenas ha sido remodelada. Sigue siendo lo que era, un piso usado para guardar muebles durante 30 años, con las paredes desempapeladas y un baño a merced de las ratas. Cabe mencionarlo: el baño *sí* ha sido reformado.

The obsession with clinging onto the past contrasts with the Ikea furniture and the plethora of gadgets. Perhaps we knew already back then that chic does not rely on wallpaper.

Der Wunsch, die Zeit anzuhalten, kollidiert mit den Ikea-Möbeln und dem Verlangen, das Ganze auszustatten. Man kann es sich kaum vorstellen: Der Schick hängt nicht von der Wandfarbe ab.

L'obsession d'arrêter le temps contraste avec les meubles Ikea et les efforts en équipement. Nous le savions déjà, le chic n'a rien à voir avec le papier peint.

La obsesión por detener el tiempo choca con el mobiliario Ikea y el afán por el equipamiento. Acaso ya lo imaginábamos: lo chic no depende del papel de las paredes.

In this renovation functionality is piled up in an explosive hodgepodge, with the bed on top of the kitchen shelves, on top of the wardrobe.

Die renovierte Hälfte erfüllt alle Funktionen einer Wohnung in einem bunten Durcheinander: Das Bett ist über den Küchenregalen über dem Kleiderschrank.

La demi-rénovation accumule toutes les fonctionnalités de la maison en un pêle-mêle explosif, comme le lit au-dessus des étagères de cuisine qui surplombent l'armoire.

La mitad reformada apila la funcionalidad de la casa en un explosivo batiburrillo: por ejemplo, la cama encima de los estantes de la cocina encima del armario de la ropa.

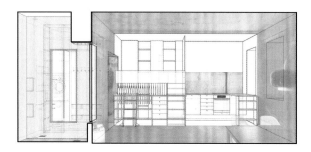
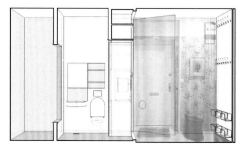

Perspectives

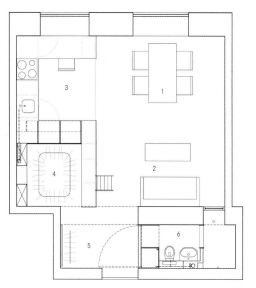

Floor plan

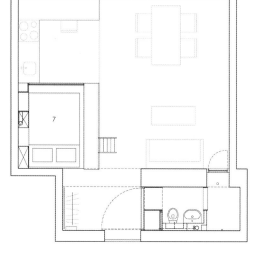

Mezzanine

1. Dinning room   5. Entrance
2. Living room   6. Bathroom
3. Kitchen   7. Bedroom
4. Dressing room

UNFOLDING APARTMENT

Normal Projects / Michael Chen Architecture
www.normalprojects.com
New York, NY, USA
420 sq ft (39 m²)
© Alan Tansey

Greater than a piece of furniture, but smaller than a piece of architecture. The challenge in this apartment was to incorporate both a workspace and an entertainment space into a smaller-than-average studio. The solution was found in extreme density and flexibility: a single piece of furniture placed along the entire length of the wall.

Viel größer als ein Möbelstück, viel kleiner als die Architektur. Die Herausforderung bei dieser Wohnung bestand in der Eingliederung aller Aspekte eines Raums, der einerseits zum Arbeiten genutzt wird, anderseits aber auch zur Unterhaltung und dies in einem Studio begrenzter Größe. Die Lösung bestand in einer extrem kompensierten Strategie und Flexibilität: ein einziges Möbelstück, das die ganze Breite der Wand einnimmt.

Plus grand qu'un meuble, plus petit que l'architecture. Dans cet appartement, le défi était d'incorporer tous les aspects d'un espace de travail et de loisirs dans un studio à taille réduite. La solution est une stratégie d'une densité et d'une flexibilité extrêmes : une seule pièce de mobilier encastrée tout au long du mur.

Más grande que un mueble, más pequeño que la arquitectura. El reto en este apartamento era incorporar todos los aspectos de un espacio destinado al trabajo y el entretenimiento dentro de un estudio de reducido tamaño. La solución, una estrategia de extrema densidad y flexibilidad: una sola pieza de mobiliario insertada lo largo de toda la pared.

The interior living space is adjusted via a series of movable doors and panels that slide and pivot, transforming it for a variety of different uses.

Der Innenbereich des Raums passt sich durch eine veränderbare Abfolge von Türen und Paneelen, die sich rollen und drehen lassen, an den jeweils gewünschten Zweck an.

L'espace intérieur s'adapte par une série modulable de portes et panneaux coulissants et pivotants. Le logement se transforme en fonction des différents usages.

El espacio interior de la vivienda se ajusta a través de una serie configurable de puertas y paneles que se deslizan y pivotan, transformándola para diversos usos.

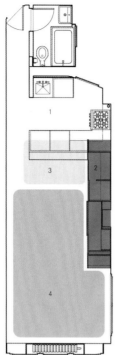

1. Kitchen
2. Closet
3. Dining room
4. Living room

Living space configuration

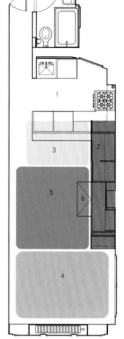

1. Kitchen
2. Closet
3. Dining room
4. Living room
5. Hall
6. Bar

Party space configuration

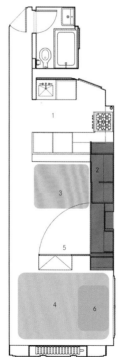

1. Kitchen
2. Closet
3. Dressing room
4. Living room
5. Screen
6. Guest bed

Guest space configuration

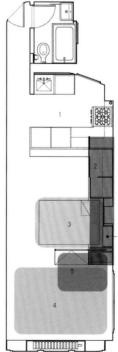

1. Kitchen
2. Closet
3. Bed
4. Living room
5. Office

Sleep space configuration

40 SQM APARTMENT

SFARO Architects
www.sfaro.co.il
Tel-Aviv, Israel
430 sq ft (40 m²)
© Boaz Lavi and Jonathan Blum

The owner of this apartment needed more space, but Tel Aviv has become prohibitively expensive and it was impossible to buy another property. The solution to this problem was to convert her existing home into a living jigsaw. Concealed within the central core are sliding doors that divide the space. The reward for solving the puzzle is clarity.

Die Besitzerin dieser Wohnung benötigte mehr Platz. Da aber in Tel Aviv die Preise unerschwinglich sind, konnte sie sich keine andere Wohnung leisten. Die Lösung bestand in diesem Kopfzerbrecher, der ihre Wohnung wortwörtlich in ein Puzzle verwandelte. Der innere Kasten verbirgt die Türen, die den Raum unterteilen. Löst jemand das Puzzle, besteht die Belohnung im Durchblick.

La propriétaire de cet appartement avait besoin de plus d'espace, mais les logements sont devenus hors de prix à Tel-Aviv ; impossible donc pour elle de s'en acheter un autre. La solution à ce casse-tête a été sa transformation en puzzle. Le noyau central dissimule les portes coulissantes qui distribuent l'espace. La récompense au bout du puzzle est la clarté.

La dueña de este apartamento necesitaba más espacio, pero en Tel Aviv los precios han ido haciéndose prohibitivos: imposible comprarse otro. La solución a este quebradero de cabeza fue, precisamente, convertir su vivienda en un rompecabezas. El núcleo central esconde las puertas correderas que distribuyen el espacio. Cuando uno resuelve el puzle, la recompensa es la diafanidad.

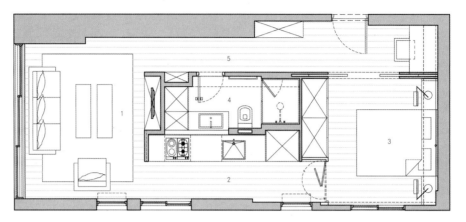

Floor plan

1. Living room
2. Kitchen
3. Bedroom
4. Barthroom
5. Corridor

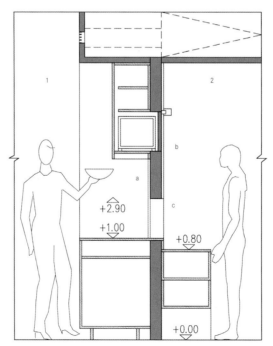

Kitchen/Bathroom section

1. Kitchen
2. Bathroom

A. Frosted glass
B. Mirror
C. Shelf

The core envelops the bathroom and storeroom, holds the kitchen, hugs the bedroom and even divides the bookcases of the hallway and lounge. The house orbits itself.

Der Kasten umschließt das Bad, einen Abstellraum, Küche und das Schlafzimmer. Die beiden Seitenwände sind Regale im Flur und im Wohnzimmer. Um ihn herum kreist die Wohnung.

Le noyau inclut la salle de bains et un débarras, soutient la cuisine, embrasse la chambre et fend les étagères du couloir et le salon. La maison tourne autour.

El núcleo encierra el baño y un trastero, sostiene la cocina, abraza el dormitorio y hasta tiene hendidos los estantes del pasillo y el salón. A su alrededor, la casa orbita.

Infinity inside a circle. The hub creates four areas with a passage around them: 360 degrees that make this apartment appear *larger* than it *is*.

Man braucht einen Kreis für das Unendliche. Durch den Würfel entstehen vier Bereiche und ein Flur: 360 Grad machen diese Wohnung zu mehr, als sie zu sein scheint.

On ne peut se servir d'un cercle pour atteindre l'infini. Le cube génère quatre zones et un parcours, 360° qui rendent cet appartement plus grand qu'il ne l'*est*.

No hay como valerse de un círculo para lograr el infinito. El cubo genera cuatro zonas y un recorrido: 360 grados que hacen que este apartamento *sea* mayor de lo que *es*.

Magicians never reveal their tricks. The doors, including their frames, merge with their environment and disappear. The mechanisms of this changing house remain hidden from us.

Ein Zauberer verrät seine Tricks nicht. Die Türen und Türrahmen verschmelzen mit der Umgebung, so dass sie verschwinden. Die Mechanismen der Wohnung bleiben für uns verborgen.

Les magiciens ne révèlent pas leurs tours. Les portes et leurs encadrements se fondent et disparaissent. Les mécanismes de la maison changeante restent cachés.

Un mago no revela sus trucos. Las puertas, incluso los marcos, se funden con el entorno para desaparecer. Los mecanismos de la casa cambiante nos permanecen ocultos.

70

MANHATTAN MICRO LOFT

Specht Harpman Architects
www.spechtharpman.com
New York, NY, USA
430 sq ft (40 m²)
© Taggart Sorenson

This apartment had a surface area of just 430 sq ft, contrasting with a seven metre-high ceiling. To make the most of the space the architects did away with individual rooms, leaving only the bathroom contained within walls. The house is a series of platforms that scale its heights. While walls often do not last in minimalist apartments, such naked space is truly daring.

Diese Wohnung hat eine Grundfläche von nur 40 m², im Gegensatz dazu aber eine Decke von 7 Metern Höhe. Um den Raum auszunutzen, trauten sich die Architekten, auf Zimmer zu verzichten. Nur das Bad befindet sich zwischen vier Wänden: Das Haus besteht aus Plattformen, die innerhalb des Raums nach oben steigen. Nun gut... Wände halten es in einer minimalistischen Wohnung nicht lange aus. Eine große Nüchternheit wirkt jedoch ungestüm.

Cet appartement ne mesurait que 40 m² au sol, avec une hauteur sous plafond de 7 m. Pour profiter de ce volume, les architectes ont osé supprimer les chambres. La salle de bains est la seule à être cloisonnée. Ce logement est une série de plateformes en escalade. Les cloisons n'ont pas la vie longue dans un appartement minimaliste. Par contre, une telle nudité est viscérale.

Este apartamento tenía una superficie de solo 40 m² y, en cambio, un techo a 7 m de altura. Para aprovechar el volumen, los arquitectos se atrevieron a prescindir de las habitaciones. Solo el cuarto de baño está entre cuatro paredes: la casa son plataformas que escalan el lugar. Bueno... las paredes no suelen durar mucho en un apartamento minimalista. Pero tamaña desnudez es visceral.

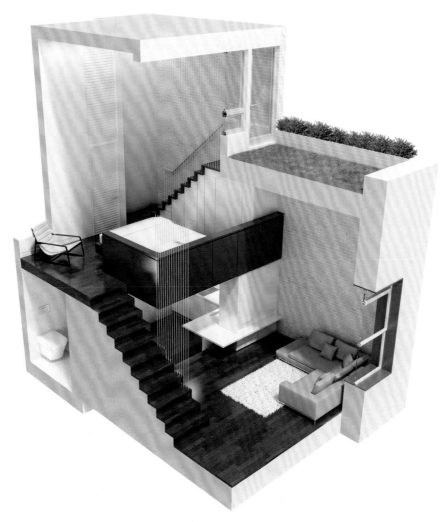

Computer generated 3D section

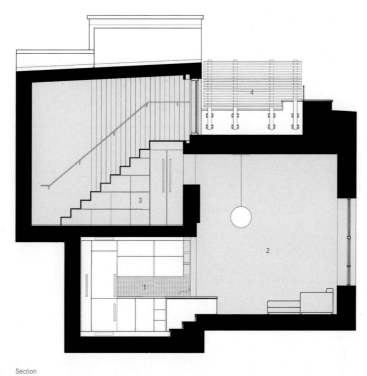

Section

1. Kitchen
2. Living room
3. Bedroom
4. Terrace

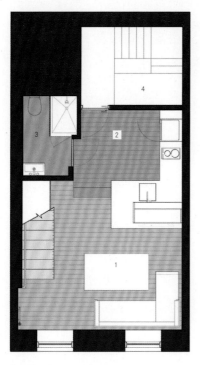

Ground floor plan

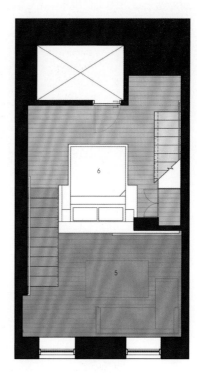

First floor plan

1. Living room
2. Kitchen
3. Bathroom
4. Stairs
5. Double volume
6. Bedroom

This central Manhattan apartment is located at the top of a six-storey building. It even has a garden, although of course it is situated on its roof.

Diese Wohnung mitten in Manhattan liegt im oberen Bereich eines Gebäudes mit sechs Stockwerken. Hier gibt es sogar einen Garten, der sich aber leider auf dem Dach befindet.

Cet appartement au cœur de Manhattan est situé tout en haut d'un immeuble à six étages. Il a même un jardin, qui se trouve forcément sur la toiture.

Este apartamento en medio de Manhattan está emplazado en lo alto de un edificio de seis pisos. Tiene incluso jardín, pero, inevitablemente, lo tiene en el tejado.

URBAN TAKE ON
MELLOW MONOCHROME

Fanny Abbes, The New Design Project
www.thenewdesignproject.com
New York, NY, USA
430 sq ft (40 m^2)
© Alan Gastelum

Modest and neutral, yet cosy and inviting. Every aspect of this New York apartment's design was focused on minimalism, yet it does not skimp on personality and individuality thanks to its wide variety of cohesive elements. A monochrome palette, recycled objects and wooden highlights lend a feeling of elegant warmth and simplicity to the space.

Bescheiden und neutral, aber freundlich und ansprechend. Der gesamte Entwurf für dieses hübsche Apartment in New York zielte darauf ab, alles auf ein Minimum zu reduzieren, Trotzdem mangelt es sich durch die verschiedenen Einzelstücke nicht an Charakter und Individualität. Eine monochromatische Palette, wieder verwendete Elemente und Akzente aus Holz und Metall verleihen dem Raum eine warme und schlichte Eleganz.

Modeste et neutre, mais accueillant et attirant. L'intervention architecturale est minimale dans ce bel appartement new-yorkais, mais elle ne lésine pas sur le caractère et l'individualité, à l'aide d'une grande variété de pièces décoratives. Une palette monochrome, des éléments réutilisés et des touches de bois et métal créent un espace d'une élégance simple et chaleureuse.

Modesto y neutro, pero acogedor y atractivo. Todo el diseño desarrollado para este bello apartamento neoyorquino ha buscado reducirse al mínimo. Sin embargo, no escatima en carácter e individualidad mediante una amplia variedad de piezas de cohesión. Una paleta monocromática, elementos reutilizados y acentos de madera y metal inyectan una elegancia cálida y sencilla al espacio.

The black and white prints, white and gold ceramics and large hand-made wood frame were all commissioned from The New Design Project.

Die Drucke in schwarz und weiß, die weiß-goldene Keramik und der große, handgemachte Metallrahmen sind vom The New Design Project in Auftrag gegebene Stücke.

Les imprimés en noir et blanc, la céramique blanc et or et le grand cadre en bois fait main sont des créations commandées par The New Design Project.

Las impresiones en blanco y negro, la cerámica blanco y oro y el gran marco de madera hecho a mano son todas creaciones encargadas por de The New Design Project.

THE TINY TRANSFORMING APARTMENT IN THE BRICK HOUSE

Eva Bradáčová
www.ebarch.cz
Prague, Czech Republic
452 sq ft (42 m²)
© Jiří Ernest

When this apartment was passed on from grandparents to grandson it needed some renovation, but nothing major. As it turned out, all that was needed to breathe modern life into these cosy brick walls was a little wise investment in the bathroom, the kitchen and the floors. Oh, and to demolish a few partitions. They only needed one bedroom: the benefits of a flat for a young couple *without* children.

Einverstanden: Als die Enkel die Wohnung von den Großeltern erbten, musste renoviert werden... aber nichts Altes bitte. Für eine moderne Lebensweise zwischen gemütlichen Seitenwänden muss man nur das Geld geschickt investieren: im Bad, der Küche und den Böden. Nun gut, ein paar Wände wurden eingerissen. Es wurde nur ein Schlafzimmer benötigt: Der Vorteile einer Wohnung für ein junges Paar *ohne* Kinder.

Héritage des grands-parents, l'appartement du petit-fils a requis un peu de rénovation, mais rien de pharaonique. Afin de faire entrer la vie moderne entre ces murs en brique, il a fallu investir intelligemment, dans la salle de bains, la cuisine et les sols. Et abattre des cloisons. Une seule chambre fut nécessaire, avantage d'un logement conçu pour un jeune couple *sans* enfants.

De acuerdo: cuando el apartamento pasó de los abuelos al nieto, requirió de cierta renovación... pero nada faraónico. Resulta que para meter la vida moderna entre algunas acogedoras paredes de ladrillo solo hizo falta invertir el dinero sabiamente: en el baño, la cocina y los suelos. Y bueno, se derribaron tabiques. Se necesitaba solo un dormitorio: ventajas de un piso para una pareja joven *sin* hijos.

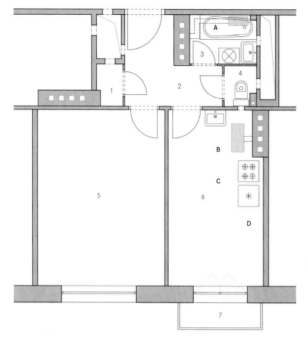

1. Storage room
2. Hall
3. Bathroom
4. Toilet
5. Bedroom
6. Kitchen
7. Balcony

A. Gas water heater
B. Heater
C. Cooker
D. Fridge

Original floor plan

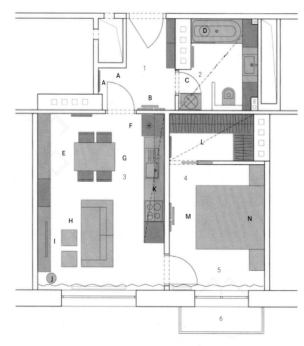

1. Hall
2. Bathroom
3. Living room/Kitchen
4. Wardrobe
5. Bedroom
6. Balcony

A. Mirror
B. Photos
C. Washing machine
D. Bathtub with shower
E. Working desk
F. Retro fridge
G. Dining table
H. Sofa
I. TV
J. Statue
K. Stone wall
L. Mirror
M. Photos/Pictures
N. Stone wall

Project floor plan

The bedroom has a minimalist feel, with nothing more than a bed. There is no need for wardrobes thanks to the separate dressing room. One less thing to worry about.

Das Schlafzimmer hat einen minimalistischen Charakter: Hier steht nur ein Bett und dank der gesonderten Garderobe der Wohnung waren auch keine Schränke nötig. Na dann gute Nacht.

La chambre présente un caractère minimaliste, meublée uniquement d'un lit et dépourvue d'armoires, grâce à la penderie située en dehors de la pièce. Elle n'est que repos.

El dormitorio tiene alma minimalista: sin más mobiliario que la cama, y despreocupado de armarios gracias al guardarropa separado de la habitación. Sosiega.

HOME 08

i29 I interior architects
www.i29.nl
Amsterdam, Netherlands
485 sq ft (45 m2)
© i29 I interior architects

It is a human trait that when we have to organise our rooms everything goes into the closet: we take everything that shouldn't be seen and we hide it away. The same is true here, where the 484 sq ft space demands to be kept clear. In this case the closets are two wooden walls that take on the very functions of the house. A table, a wardrobe, a fireplace. Everything counts.

Es ist ein menschlicher Wohnraum. Wenn wir eine Wohnung aufräumen müssen, locken uns Schränke: Wir nehmen alles, was nicht mehr in Sichtweite sein soll und legen es hinein. Hier ist es genau dasselbe: Eine Grundfläche von nur 45 m² zwingt einfach dazu, aufzuräumen. Die Schränke sind in diesem Fall aus Holz, in denen sich *alle* Funktionen des Hauses befinden. Bank oder Kleiderschrank. Oder ein Kamin: Alles vorhanden.

C'est humain. Quand on doit ranger une pièce, les armoires nous invitent à ramasser tout ce qui ne devrait pas être visible et l'y mettre. C'est la même chose ici ; une surface de 45 m² seulement oblige à dégager l'espace. Deux cloisons en bois qui remplissent *toutes* les fonctions de la maison font office d'armoires. Un banc ou la penderie. Ou une cheminée, peu importe.

Es un hábito humano. Cuando tenemos que recoger una habitación, los armarios nos tientan: arramblar con todo lo que no debería quedar a la vista y meterlo para dentro. Aquí es lo misma: una superficie de solo 45 m² impone despejar el espacio. Los armarios, esta vez, son dos paredes de madera que acogen *todas* las funciones de la casa. Un banco o el guardarropa. O una chimenea: tanto da.

"We try to design the space, focusing on the absence of what is physically there", explain the architects. "And that can only be achieved by designing the physical."

„Unsere Absicht bestand darin, den Raum zu entwerfen: Die Abwesenheit dessen, was physisch anwesend ist", sagen die Architekten. "Und das kann man nur erreichen, wenn man das Physische auch entwirft."

« Nous essayons de dessiner l'espace, l'absence de ce qui est physiquement là, disent les architectes. On n'y arrive qu'en dessinant ce qui est physique. »

"Lo que intentamos es diseñar el espacio: la ausencia de lo que está físicamente ahí", dicen los arquitectos. "Y eso solo se puede lograr diseñando lo físico."

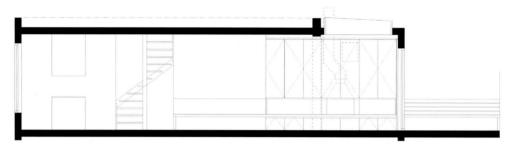

Section a-a

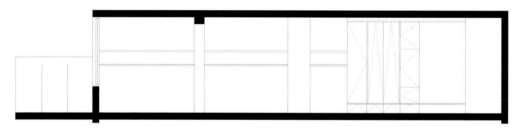

Section b-b

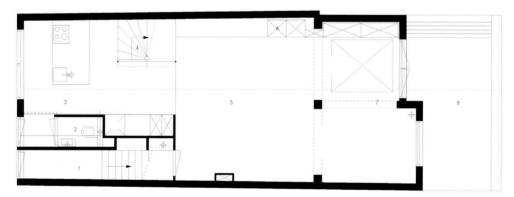

Floor plan

1. Entrance
2. Toilet
3. Kitchen
4. Stairs
5. Hall
6. Fireplace
7. Living room
8. Patio

BARN LOFT

Fabrizio Miccò Architetti Associati
www.fmaa.it
Rome, Italy
485 sq ft (45 m2)
© Fabrizio Miccò

Here we have an antique box for modern invention. The first is a mediaeval granary on the outskirts of Rome. The second, a radical, minimalist structure that is a "discrete but not mimetic guest of the building" (say the architects). It is not so much about discretion however, but more akin the curious ability of hermit crabs to adapt to their shell.

Dies ist ein alter Hut für eine moderne Erfindung. Das erste ist eine mittelalterliche Scheune in der Umgebung von Rom. Das zweite ist eine minimalistische Struktur mit radikaler Seele, die „als diskreter, jedoch nicht mimetischer Gast" im Gebäude Wirkung tut (laut dem Studio). Es scheint jedoch nicht wirklich diskret zu sein. Vielmehr die seltsame Fähigkeit der Einsiedlerkrebse, sich an ihre Schale anzupassen.

On a ici une vieille boîte pour une nouvelle invention. La première est un grenier médiéval dans la banlieue de Rome. La deuxième est une structure minimaliste à l'âme radicale, qui joue « l'invité discret mais pas mimétique » de l'édifice, selon l'agence. Cela n'a pas l'air discret, justement. Il s'agit plutôt de la curieuse capacité d'un bernard-l'ermite à s'adapter à sa coquille.

He aquí una caja antigua para un invento moderno. Lo primero es un granero medieval a las afueras de Roma. Lo segundo, una estructura minimalista, de alma radical, que hace de "invitado discreto aunque no mimético" (dicen desde el estudio) del edificio. Pero no parece discreción precisamente. Más bien la curiosa capacidad de los cangrejos ermitaños para adaptarse a su concha.

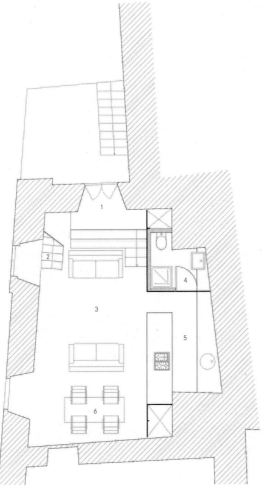

Ground floor plan

1. Entrance
2. Stairs
3. Living room
4. Bathroom
5. Kitchen
6. Dining room

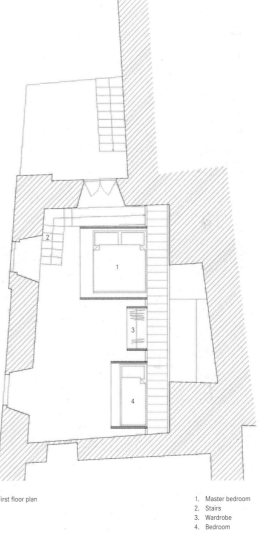

First floor plan

1. Master bedroom
2. Stairs
3. Wardrobe
4. Bedroom

The sleeping area represents the most visceral form within this loft, with its three cages suspended in the air. This is for people who are committed to aesthetics.

Der Schlafbereich nimmt die ungestümste Form an, die man in diesem Loft finden kann: Drei Käfige hängen in der Luft. Für Bewohner, die sich mit der Ästhetik des Ortes engagieren.

L'espace nuit adopte la forme la plus viscérale de ce *loft*, trois cages suspendues en l'air. Pour des résidents en phase avec l'esthétique du lieu.

La zona para dormir adopta la forma más visceral que se puede encontrar en este *loft*: tres jaulas suspendidas en el aire. Para residentes comprometidos con la estética del lugar.

G-ROC

Nook Architects
www.nookarchitects.com
Barcelona, Spain
495 sq ft (46 m²)
© nieve | Productora Audiovisual

Nook Architects' work on this property reclaims and strengthens the building's original spirit, subtly intervening in the resulting space. The kitchen is located in the noisiest part of the building. On the other hand the sleeping area makes the most of the height, having been divided cleanly into two, linked by a gallery to the terrace where the bathroom is situated.

Die Arbeit von Nook Architects in dieser Wohnung brachte wieder den ursprünglichen Geist des Gebäudes zurück und verankerte ihn, so dass er sich im so entstandenen Raum ausbreiten kann. Die Küche befindet sich in geräuschvollsten Teil der Finca. Andererseits wurde im Schlafbereich die Höhe vergrößert und in zwei Ebenen unterteilt und die Galerie verbindet sich nun mit der kleinen Terrasse, wo sich das Bad befindet.

Ici, le travail de Nook Architects récupère et consolide l'esprit d'origine de l'édifice, en intervenant subtilement dans l'espace résultant. La cuisine est située dans la partie la plus bruyante. La hauteur de l'espace nuit est renforcée lorsqu'elle est occasionnellement divisée en deux. L'espace de la galerie est relié à la petite terrasse qui inclut la salle de bains.

La labor de Nook Architects en esta vivienda recupera y consolida el espíritu original del edificio, interviniendo sutilmente en el espacio resultante. La cocina se ubica en la parte más ruidosa de la finca. Por otro lado, en la zona de noche, se potencia la altura al dividirla puntualmente en dos, y se vincula el espacio de galería a la pequeña terraza donde se sitúa el baño.

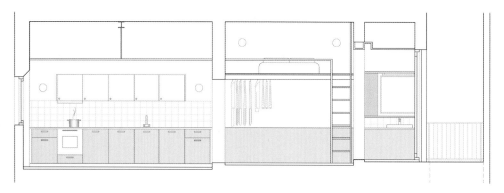

Section

Floor plan

1. Kitchen   A. Day area
2. Mezzanine B. Night area
3. Bathroom
4. Terrace

The construction of the loft was key within the project, creating an upstairs bedroom and freeing up space on the ground floor to be used as a studio, lounge or dressing room.

Die Konstruktion des Zwischengeschoss, sozusagen das Schlüsselelements des Projekts, ermöglicht die Unterbringung eines Betts im oberen Teil und macht so den unteren Teil frei für andere Dinge, wie zum Beispiel ein Studio, ein Wohnzimmer oder ein Ankleidezimmer.

L'inclusion de la mezzanine, une partie clé du projet, permet d'y poser un lit et de libérer le niveau inférieur pouvant servir d'atelier, séjour et vestiaire.

La construcción del altillo, clave en el proyecto, permite ubicar una cama arriba y liberar la planta inferior, que puede usarse como estudio, sala de estar o vestidor.

BREAK APARTMENT

Tavares Duayer Arquitetura
www.tavaresduayer.com.br
Rio de Janeiro, Brazil
516 sq ft (48 m^2)
© André Nazareth © João Duayer

In this small apartment, every design element has a specific purpose. From the different materials used to the colours of the walls and furniture, everything was chosen in order to create a backdrop against which the owner could display the many objects from his various collections.

In diesem kleinen Apartment haben alle Design-Elemente ein bestimmtes Ziel: Die verschiedenen verwendeten Materialien, die Farben der Wände und der Möbel wurden alle ausgewählt, um das Hintergrundszenario für die zahlreichen Objekte der verschiedenen Kollektionen zu bilden, die der Besitzer ausstellen wollte.

Dans ce petit appartement, tous les éléments architecturaux ont un but précis. Les différents matériaux utilisés, ainsi que les couleurs des murs et des meubles, ont été choisis comme toile de fond pour permettre au propriétaire d'exposer les multiples objets qui composent ses collections diverses.

En este pequeño apartamento, todos los elementos de diseño tienen un fin concreto: los diferentes materiales utilizados, los colores de las paredes y los muebles, todos fueron elegidos al servicio del escenario en que el propietario pudiera exponer los múltiples objetos de sus diversas colecciones.

The pipe work has been left partially visible.
Combined with the grey tones, wood and brick,
it creates a contemporary and industrial feel.

Das teilweise verborgene Rohrsystem, die
grauen Farbtöne, das Holz und die Ziegel
sorgen für einen modernen Industriestil.

La tuyauterie partiellement visible se marie aux
tons gris, au bois et à la brique afin de créer un
style contemporain et industriel.

La tubería, dejada parcialmente a la vista,
combinada con los tonos grises, la madera y el
ladrillo proporcionan un estilo contemporáneo
e industrial.

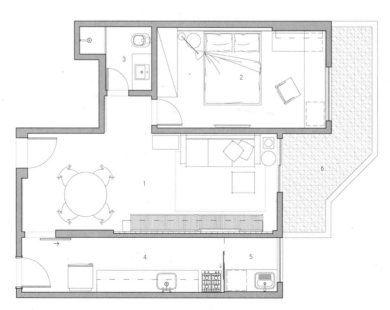

1. Living room
2. Bedroom
3. Bathroom
4. Kitchen
5. Laundry
6. Balcony

Floor plan

LOW-BUDGET APARTMENT

Studio 8 1/2
www.studio812.eu
Plovdiv, Bulgaria
540 sq ft (50 m²)
© Vladislav Kostadinov

This apartment was being renovated for rental, so the architects had the bare minimum to work with: a budget of only 500 Euros, a timescale of just a month and no specific client to adapt the design to. The result was a very personal interpretation of the meaning of modern life. It was also a lavish tribute to low-cost design.

Die Renovierung dieser Wohnung wurde durchgeführt, bevor sie vermietet wurde. Daher musste das Studio mit weniger als dem Minimum auskommen: 500 Euro als Budget, einen Monat Zeit und die Unmöglichkeit, sich an den Bewohner anzupassen, da es keinen gab. Was dabei herauskam, war eine sehr persönliche Interpretation dessen, was das moderne Leben ausmacht. Und eine prunkvolle Hommage an das *low-cost*-Design.

Le but de la restructuration de cet appartement était la location. L'agence a donc dû s'en sortir avec le minimum, un budget de 500 euros, un délai d'un mois et l'impossibilité de s'adapter au locataire, car il n'y en avait aucun. Le résultat fut une interprétation très personnelle de la vie moderne. Cela, et encore un hommage fastueux au design *low-cost*.

La remodelación de este apartamento se llevó a cabo para alquilar la vivienda, así que el estudio tuvo que salir adelante con menos de lo mínimo: 500 euros de presupuesto, un mes de plazo y la imposibilidad de adaptarse al huésped, ya que no había ninguno. Lo que surgió fue una interpretación muy personal de lo que es la vida moderna. Eso, y un fastuoso homenaje al diseño *low-cost*.

The architects designed the furnishings. They may be recycled but they are new ideas. Repainting old furniture is one thing, but giving it a completely new function within the house is quite another.

Das Studio entwarf das Mobiliar. Es handelt sich nur um Recycling: Es sind Ideen. Ein altes Möbelstück anstreichen ist eine Sache. Ihm eine neue Funktion innerhalb der Wohnung zu geben, eine andere, vielleicht noch wichtigere Sache.

Le mobilier est conçu en agence. C'est plus que du recyclage. Peindre un vieux meuble est une chose ; lui donner une nouvelle fonction en est une autre, plus importante encore.

El estudio diseñó el mobiliario. No solo es reciclar: son ideas. Pintar un mueble viejo es una parte. Darle una nueva función dentro de la casa es otra, más importante aún.

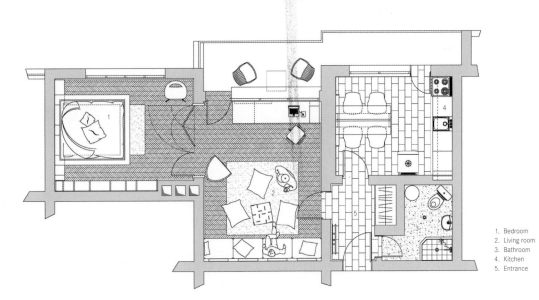

Floor plan

1. Bedroom
2. Living room
3. Bathroom
4. Kitchen
5. Entrance

The use of cardboard is not concealed. The apartment proudly shows off its low-budget nature, such as the recycled bottles. Nothing is hidden.

Es gibt zwar Karton, aber keine Tricks: In der Wohnung ist ohne Scheu die Natürlichkeit des geringen Budgets zur Schau gestellt. Wie zum Beispiel die recycelten Flaschen. Nichts bleibt verborgen.

Il y a du carton, mais pas de tromperie. L'appartement exhibe son petit budget sans complexe. Les bouteilles recyclées, par exemple, qui ne cachent rien.

Hay cartón, pero no trampa: el apartamento exhibe sin complejos su naturaleza de bajo presupuesto. Las botellas recicladas, por ejemplo. No esconden nada.

SOSPESO

Studioata
www.studioata.com
Turin, Italy
540 sq ft (50 m²)
© Barbara Corsico

In an elegant building in central Turin, Studioata's design separates off a small section of this large apartment to make it independent from the rest. What we are left with is a large space, born from the union of two rooms and the entrance lobby, articulated around a large, central shape.

In einem Herrenhaus im Zentrum von Turin wird im Entwurf von Studioata ein kleiner Teil eines Apartments abgetrennt, um ihn vom Rest der Wohnung abzugrenzen. So entsteht ein einzigartiger, großer Raum aus der Vereinigung zweier Zimmer und des Eingangsbereichs, die durch den großen zentralen Raum miteinander verbunden werden: Das ist die Grundfläche des Projekts.

Dans un édifice seigneurial situé au centre de Turin, l'architecture de Studioata sépare une petite partie d'un grand appartement, afin de la rendre indépendante du reste. L'ensemble du projet se compose d'un seul grand espace issu de la jonction de deux pièces et de l'espace d'entrée, articulés autour d'un grand volume central.

En un edificio señorial situado en el centro de Turín, el diseño realizado por Studioata separa una pequeña parte de un gran apartamento para independizarlo del resto. Ahora, un único gran espacio que nace de la unión de dos habitaciones y de la zona de entrada, y articuladas a partir de un gran volumen central, componen todo el espacio del proyecto.

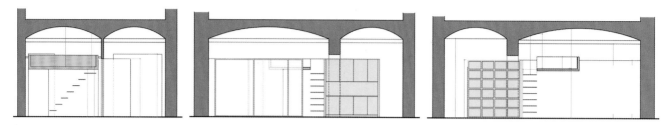

Sections

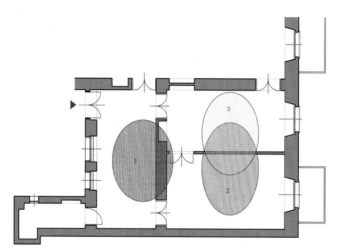

Concept plan

1. Entrance
2. Night area
3. Day area

A. Identity at the entrance. Use and exploit the expansion area of entry to not waste
B. Free space. Collect and concentrate in an area the service space and the furniture is released and expands the usable space
C. Flexibility. Create communication between the living and sleeping areas to define an expanded space and changed depending on

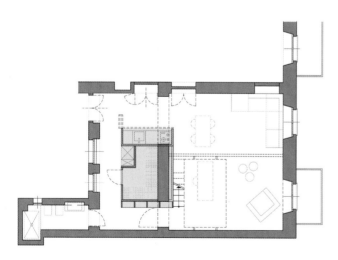

Floor plan

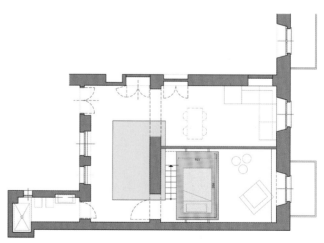

Mezzanine floor plan

In order to free up as much space as possible, the bed is hidden inside a hanging module, accessible via a lightweight metal ladder.

Das Ziel bestand darin, so viel Raum wie möglich zu schaffen. Das Bett verbirgt sich in dem in der Luft hängenden Zimmer, zu dem man über eine Treppe aus Leichtmetall gelangt.

Afin de dégager le plus d'espace possible, le lit est dissimulé derrière le volume suspendu, auquel on accède par un escalier en métal léger.

Con el fin de liberar tanto espacio como sea posible, la cama se encuentra oculta dentro del volumen suspendido, accesible por una escalera de metal ligero.

The central module unites and organises the three areas of the studio, and houses a dressing room and kitchen area, hidden behind glazed wooden panels.

Der zentrale Raum vereint und gliedert die drei Bereiche des Studios. Hier befinden sich ein Ankleidezimmer und der Küchenbereich, der hinter den verglasten Holzpaneelen verborgen ist.

Le volume central réunit et organise les trois parties du studio et contient un vestiaire et l'espace cuisine, caché derrière des panneaux en bois vitré.

El volumen central une y organiza las tres áreas del estudio y contiene un vestidor y la zona de la cocina, oculta detrás de paneles de madera acristalada.

TRANSFORMER LOFT

Studio Garneau
www.studiogarneau.com
New York, NY, USA
548 sq ft (51 m^2)
© Bart Michiels © Robert Garneau

A dilapidated pre-war studio has been transformed into a flexible and open space, creating an urban sanctuary above the frenzy of New York city. This design has created a clean and simple refuge full of light and space, without the visual obstruction of possessions: a place that offers functionality and the ability to get on with day-to-day routines.

Ein Studio, das vor dem Krieg eine Ruine war, wurde in einen wandelbaren und offenen Raum verwandelt. Heraus kam ein urbaner Rückzugsort oberhalb des geschäftigen Treibens von New York. Die Lösung bei diesem Entwurf bestand in der Schaffung eines sauberen und einfachen Refugiums voller Licht und Luft und ohne die visuellen Störfaktoren der üblichen Gegenstände, das dennoch die notwendige Funktionalität mitbringt, durch die tägliche Routine möglich ist.

Un atelier d'avant-guerre, en ruine, devient un espace flexible et ouvert ; on construit un sanctuaire urbain, au-dessus de la frénésie new-yorkaise. La solution architecturale choisie crée un refuge de lumière et d'espace, sobre et simple, épargné de la gêne visuelle que créent les objets. Il offre pourtant la fonctionnalité nécessaire et rend possible la routine quotidienne.

Un estudio en ruinas anterior a la guerra se transforma en un espacio flexible y abierto; se crea un santuario urbano por encima del frenesí de la ciudad de Nueva York. La solución de su diseño crea un limpio y sencillo refugio de luz y espacio, sin el estorbo visual de las posesiones, que no deja de ofrecer la funcionalidad necesaria y que permite las rutinas diarias.

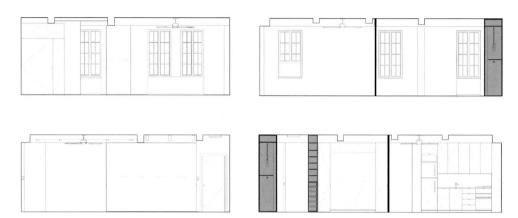

Sections

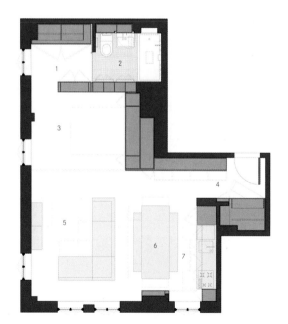

Floor plan

1. Dressing room   5. Living room
2. Bathroom   6. Dining room
3. Bedroom   7. Kitchen
4. Entrance

By sliding a wall the bedroom is separated from the lounge, whilst revealing a library or office right here in the house. The result is personal and customised.

Eine Wand, die verschoben werden kann, trennt das Schlafzimmer vom Wohnzimmer und enthüllt je nach Position eine Bibliothek oder ein Büro. Das Ergebnis: ein ganz individueller Raum.

Une cloison coulissante sépare la chambre du séjour et dévoile aussi la bibliothèque et le bureau de la maison. Le résultat en est une ambiance personnalisée.

Deslizar una pared separa el dormitorio de la sala de estar, al tiempo que revela una biblioteca o una oficina en casa. El resultado: un entorno personalizado.

SAL HOUSE

Nook Architects
www.nookarchitects.com
Barcelona, Spain
613 sq ft (57 m²)
© nieve I Productora audiovisual

The designers of the Nook had to navigate a storm on their voyage from small to chic. The geometry of the space and the minimalist size of this 19 x 3 m rectangle were a major problem. And then came the terrace, worn out, uneven and disconnected from the building. The architects had no hesitation in putting the owner at the helm of the project. The house was made for her.

Bei der großen Entfernung, die vom Kleinen zum Schicken reicht, hatten die Designer von Nook mit Gegenwind zu kämpfen. Die Geometrie des Ortes, der alles andere als klein ist, war unbequem: ein Rechteck mit fast 19 x 3 Meter. Und dann war da noch die Terrasse: abgenutzt, uneben und nicht gut an den Rest der Wohnung angebunden. Das Studio ließ keinen Zweifel aufkommen: Die Besitzerin ist die Steuerfrau des Projekts. Die Wohnung wurde für sie geschaffen.

Les designers new-yorkais ont pris un chemin semé d'embûches pour rendre chic ce qui n'était que mignon. La géométrie du lieu était petite et inconfortable, un rectangle d'à peine 19 m sur 3 m. Et puis il y avait la terrasse usée, dénivelée et un peu décalée du reste du logement. L'agence n'a pas hésité à mettre la propriétaire aux manettes de ce projet. La maison a été faite pour elle.

En la larga travesía que va de lo pequeño a lo chic, los diseñadores de Nook se las tuvieron que ver con vendavales. La geometría del lugar, además de pequeña, era incómoda: un rectángulo de apenas 19 x 3 metros. Y luego estaba la terraza: desgastada, desnivelada y mal conectada al hogar. El estudio no lo dudó: puso a la propietaria de timonel del proyecto. La casa se hizo para ella.

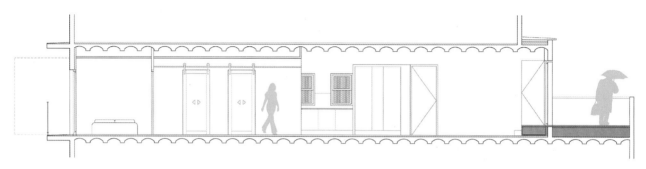

Section

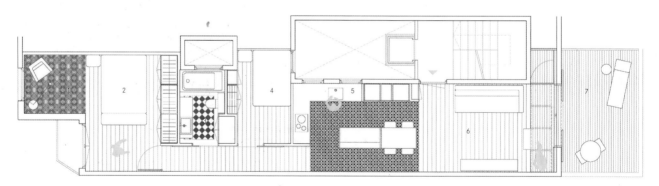

Floor plan

1. Study
2. Master bedroom
3. Bathroom
4. Bedroom
5. Kitchen
6. Living room
7. Terrace

For the owner, the most important aspect was the kitchen. The architects met her wishes: more than being the house's kitchen, the house is where this kitchen lives.

Für die Eigentümerin war die Küche das Wichtigste. Das Studio erfüllte ihr den Wunsch. Dieser Raum ist weitaus mehr als die Küche der Wohnung, dieser Raum ist die Wohnung der Küche.

Pour la propriétaire la cuisine était très importante. L'agence a répondu à ses vœux : plus que la cuisine de la maison, ce lieu est la maison de cette cuisine.

Para la propietaria de la vivienda, lo más importante era la cocina. El estudio la complació: más que la cocina de esta casa, el lugar es la casa de esta cocina.

The renovation began by attacking the façade
and opening the isolated terrace to the lounge.
The uneven levels were tamed within the
house, creating a staircase, breakfast bar and
library.

Der Umbau stürmte auf die Fassade ein: Die
Terrasse wurde Teil des Wohnzimmer. Das
Gefälle wurde in die Wohnung geholt und dient
nun als Stufen, Bank und Bibliothek.

On a commencé la rénovation en s'attaquant
à la façade et en ouvrant la terrasse isolée
sur le salon. On a maîtrisé la dénivellation
en la convertissant en escalier, en banc et
en bibliothèque.

La reforma arremetió contra la fachada: abrió
la aislada terraza al salón. El desnivel se
domesticó dentro de casa, convirtiéndolo en
unas escaleras, banco y librería.

APARTMENT FOR RENT IN MILAN

studioWOK
www.studiowok.com
Milan, Italy
700 sq ft (65 m²)
© Federico Villa

A house renovated especially for you. And for anyone else in fact. This is a rental flat and needs to meet the needs of every possible client. Its flexibility comes from the comfortable communal areas: space, white to increase the light, some wood floors, etc. It may not be *your* dream home but you have to admit you could live in it quite comfortably.

Eine renovierte Wohnung nur für Sie. Und für jede andere Person: Es handelt sich um eine Mietwohnung, die allen potentiellen Interessenten gefallen muss. Die Flexibilität schlägt in den gemeinschaftlichen genutzten Zimmern den Komfort: Der Raum ist weiß, um mehr Licht auszustrahlen, einige Böden sind aus Holz usw. Gut, vielleicht ist es nicht *Ihr* Traumhaus. Sie müssen jedoch anerkennen: Hier kann man ganz gut leben.

Una casa reformada especialmente para usted. Y para cualquier otra persona, de hecho: el apartamento es de alquiler y tiene que satisfacer a todos los hipotéticos clientes. La flexibilidad se buscó en los lugares comunes del confort: espacio, blanco para expandir la luz, algunos suelos de madera, etcétera. Bueno, tal vez no sea *su* casa soñada. Pero reconózcalo: viviría en ella tan cómodamente.

Sections

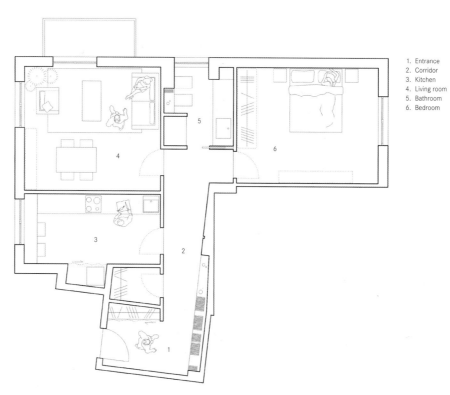

Floor plan

1. Entrance
2. Corridor
3. Kitchen
4. Living room
5. Bathroom
6. Bedroom

The renovation budget was low, but even so it makes sense. Wood flooring in the bedrooms and lounge, concrete for the rest of the house.

Das Budget für den Umbau war recht niedrig. So macht es Sinn: Holzböden für die Schlafzimmer und das Wohnzimmer, Beton für den Rest der Wohnung.

Malgré son budget plutôt bas cette rénovation tient debout : des sols en bois dans les chambres et le salon ainsi que du béton pour le reste de la maison.

El presupuesto para la remodelación era más bien bajo. Aun así, tiene sentido: suelos de madera para los dormitorios y el salón; hormigón para el resto de la casa.

The bathroom is simple but functional. No matter how appropriate, baroque touches and eccentricities are not to everyone's taste but functionality is.

Das Badezimmer ist einfach, aber funktional: Ein barocker und exzentrischer Stil (auch wenn es geeignet scheint) gefällt nicht jedem. Die Funktionalität jedoch sehr wohl.

La salle de bains est simple et fonctionnelle. Les touches baroques et les excentricités ne sont pas au goût de tout le monde, contrairement à la fonctionnalité.

El cuarto de baño es simple pero funcional: los barroquismos y las excentricidades, incluso las más oportunas, no gustan a todo el mundo. La funcionalidad, sí.

L APARTMENT

Olivier Chabaud Architecte
www.olivierchabaud.com
Paris, France
700 sq ft (65 m²)
© Philippe Harden

When there is no space to create a maze, rooms are joined one to another and, doing away with walls, space is achieved. This is what Chabaud did with this apartment, but he went even further by softening their connections. Now the lobby leans into the lounge, which opens to the kitchen and bedroom. Even the shower floats next to the bed. The connections are ethereal and pure.

Wenn man keinen Raum für Labyrinthe hat, verbinden sich die Zimmer mit einander. Verzichtet man auf Wände, kann man weit blicken. Dieses Vorgehen wählte Chabaud für diese Wohnung, ging jedoch noch einen Schritt weiter: Die Übergänge wurden geglättet. Nun öffnet sich der Eingangsbereich zum Wohnzimmer hin, der in die Küche und das Schlafzimmer übergeht. Sogar die Dusche scheint neben dem Bett zu schweben. Die Abtrennungen kann man schon ätherisch nennen.

S'il n'y a pas assez de place pour un labyrinthe, les chambres s'encastrent pour créer un espace transparent et décloisonné. C'est ce qu'a fait Chabaud avec cet appartement, tout en allant plus loin pour réduire les accès. Le hall d'entrée est repoussé vers le salon ouvert sur la cuisine et la chambre. Même la douche flotte à côté du lit. On pourrait dire de ces accès qu'ils sont aériens.

Cuando no hay espacio para amagar laberintos, las habitaciones se ensamblan las unas con las otras y, prescindiendo de paredes, se logra lo diáfano. Así lo hizo Chabaud con este apartamento, pero fue más allá: suavizó las conexiones. Ahora, el vestíbulo empuja hacia el salón, que se abre a la cocina y al dormitorio. Incluso la ducha flota al lado de la cama. Las particiones son puro etéreo.

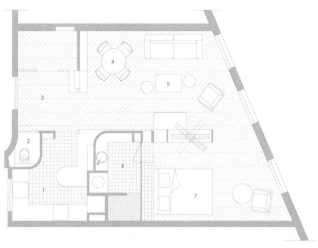

Floor plan

1. Kitchen
2. Toilet
3. Entrance
4. Dining room
5. Living room
6. Bathroom
7. Bedroom

With this unit the TV can face into the living room or the bedroom, placing itself in either room. It feels as though all the rooms inhabit the same space.

Dieses Möbelstück ermöglicht es, den Fernseher zum Wohnzimmer oder zum Schlafzimmer hin auszurichten, ihn in das eine oder andere Zimmer zu holen. Man merkt, dass die Zimmer alle denselben Raum einnehmen.

Ce meuble permet de tourner la télé vers le salon, la chambre ou la faire changer de pièce. On a l'impression que toutes les pièces habitent le même espace.

Este mueble permite encarar el televisor hacia el salón o hacia el dormitorio; meterlo en una u otra estancia. Uno siente todas las habitaciones habitando un mismo espacio.

JES HOUSE

Nook Architects
www.nookarchitects.com
Barcelona, Spain
700 sq ft (65 m²)
© nieve | Productora Audiovisual

This Barcelona apartment was a hodgepodge of equally sized rooms, making it difficult to achieve chic from such chaos. Instead of tearing down walls in search of space, the areas were tiered instead. The bedroom floor was raised, the kitchen was opened to the dining room and so on. The result demonstrates that small houses do not need eccentricity. All they need is ingenuity.

Diese Wohnung in Barcelona war ein einziges Durcheinander von Zimmern derselben Größe: Schick konnte man in dieser heillosen Unordnung nicht unterbringen. Anstatt jedoch Wände einzureißen und Raum zu schaffen, wurden alle Bereiche hierarchisch angeordnet. Der Boden des Schlafzimmers wurde erhöht, die Küche öffnet sich zum Esszimmer hin... Das Ergebnis beweist, dass kleine Häuser nicht der Exzentrik unterworfen sein müssen. Einem gewissen Erfindergeist sehr wohl.

Cet appartement barcelonais était constitué de pièces en pagaille de même dimensions. Difficile de faire du chic dans un tel désordre. Au lieu d'abattre les murs et de chercher le vide, les zones ont été hiérarchisées. Le sol de la chambre a été surélevé et la cuisine ouverte sur la salle à manger. Le résultat prouve que les petites maisons n'ont pas besoin d'extravagance. Mais d'astuce, oui !

Este apartamento barcelonés era un batiburrillo de habitaciones del mismo tamaño: difícil lograr lo chic en semejante desconcierto. En lugar de tirar paredes abajo y buscar vacíos, lo que se hizo fue jerarquizar las zonas. Se elevó el suelo del dormitorio, se abrió la cocina al comedor... El resultado demuestra que las casas pequeñas no obligan a lo excéntrico. Obligan al ingenio, eso sí.

Sections

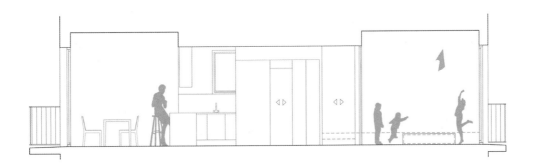

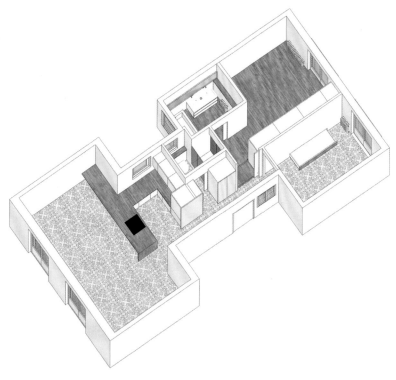

Axonometry

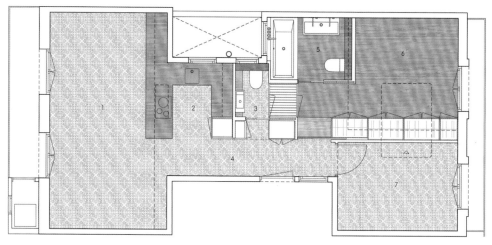

Floor plan

1. Living room
2. Kitchen
3. Toilet
4. Corridor
5. Bathroom
6. Master bedroom
7. Bedroom/Study

The guest bed works like a large-format
magic trick: the whole house needed to adapt
to it. But it can get completely lost...a whole
double bed!

Das Gästebett ist ein übergroßer magischer
Trick: Das ganze Haus musste sich ihm
anpassen. Man kann es jedoch verschwinden
lassen... das komplette Ehebett!

Le lit des invités est tel un tour de magie grand
format. Toute la maison a dû s'y adapter.
Mais cela permet de faire disparaître un lit
matrimonial en entier !

La cama de invitados funciona como un
truco de magia de gran formato: toda la casa
tuvo que adaptarse a él. Pero permite hacer
desaparecer... ¡una cama de matrimonio entera!

FLAT VILAS

Castroferro Arquitectos
www.castroferro.com
Vigo, Spain
720 sq ft (67 m²)
© Héctor Santos-Díez | BISimages

This second floor could just as well be on Mars or under the ground, because here in the city centre, its windows look out to nothing. The light is stolen by the surrounding buildings and the only two views it has, to the inside of the block and the building courtyard, horrified the designers. Thus they expanded behind closed doors instead. A pity, however, that those who dare cannot see what lies behind the windows.

Die zweite Wohnung könnte auf dem Mars oder unter der Erde sein. Sie ist dort, inmitten der Stadt, die Fenster gehen ins Nichts hinaus. Die umliegenden Gebäude nehmen das Licht und die beiden echten Ausblicke (ins Innere des Häuserblocks und auf den Hof des Gebäudes) entsetzten die Designer. Das Haus dehnt sich daher mit Hilfe von Türen ins Innere aus. Für die Wagemutigeren: Leider kann man nicht sehen, was auf der anderen Seite der Fenster befindet.

Ce deuxième niveau aurait pu se trouver sur Mars ou sur Terre, car ses fenêtres n'ont vue sur rien là où il est, en pleine ville. Les immeubles autour lui font de l'ombre. Les seules vues qu'il offre (vers l'îlot et sur la cour de l'immeuble) ont terrifié les architectes. La maison se déploie vers l'intérieur. Dommage que les plus vaillants ne puissent voir au-delà des fenêtres.

Este segundo piso podría haber estado en Marte o bajo tierra, porque allí donde está, en medio de la ciudad, las ventanas no dan a ningún sitio. Los edificios a su alrededor le quitan la luz, y las dos únicas vistas de que goza (al interior de la manzana y al patio del edificio) horrorizaron a los diseñadores. La casa se expande, pues, de puertas para adentro. Para los más atrevidos, lástima que no podamos ver lo que hay tras las ventanas.

Stripping back the wall to stone, covering the wooden floor and choosing a white lacquer for the central wall was all it took to make the inside *friendly*.

Die Wände wurden bis auf die Steine freigelegt, der Boden mit Holz bedeckt und ein weißer Lack auf der zentralen Trennwand angebracht, um das Innere des Hauses *liebenswert* zu machen.

Un mur dénudé pour atteindre la pierre, un sol revêtu de bois et le blanc laqué de la cloison centrale ont suffi pour rendre *aimable* l'intérieur de la maison.

Desnudar la pared hasta llegar a la piedra, cubrir el suelo de madera y elegir un blanco lacado para el tabique central bastó para hacer amable el *interior* de la casa.

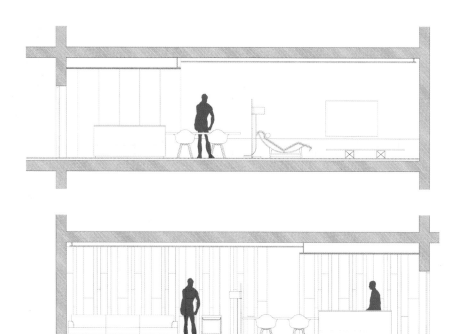

Sections

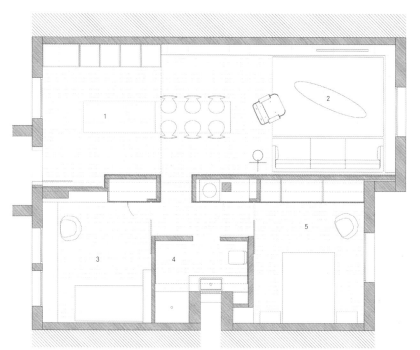

Floor plan

1. Kitchen
2. Living room
3. Bedroom
4. Bathroom
5. Master bedroom

The versatile open spaces are not only for walking in. The house itself needs them in order for the light to bounce freely from one target to another.

Die ausgedehnten Räume sind vielseitig und man hat mehr Möglichkeiten als in ihnen herumzuschlendern. Das Haus selbst erfordert es, damit das Licht nach Belieben von dem strahlenden Weiß zurückgeworfen wird.

Les espaces amples et polyvalents ne servent pas seulement à la marche. La maison en a besoin, pour que la lumière puisse rebondir d'un espace blanc à l'autre.

Los espacios amplios, versátiles, no solo sirven para andar por ellos. Los necesita la casa misma, para que la luz pueda rebotar a libertad de blanco a blanco.

UNIT #2

ras-a, inc.
www.ras-a.com
Manhattan Beach, CA, USA
720 sq ft (67 m²)
© Roel Kuiper

The elegance of this renovated apartment is centred mainly in the beautiful laminated wood cabinet. The different sections of the home were previously divided into two by a separating wall, but now revolve around the multifunctional cabinet while opening up to the beautiful views over the Pacific Ocean.

Die Eleganz dieses renovierten Apartments entsteht vor allem durch die zentrale Rolle, die der hübsche Schrank aus mit Platten verkleidetem Holz einnimmt. Die unterschiedlichen Zimmer der Wohnung, die sich ursprünglich zu beiden Seiten einer Trennwand befanden, sind heute um den multifunktionalen Schrank herum angeordnet und bieten durch die Fenster einen hübschen Blick auf den Pazifik.

L'élégance de cet appartement rénové réside principalement dans le rôle central de la belle armoire en bois laminé. Les différentes pièces du logement, auparavant réparties des deux côtés d'une cloison de séparation, tournent maintenant autour de l'armoire multifonctionnelle et s'ouvrent sur de belles vues de l'océan Pacifique.

La elegancia de este renovado apartamento reside principalmente en el papel central que juega el bello armario de madera laminada. Los diferentes ambientes de la vivienda, que anteriormente se distribuían a ambos lados de un muro de separación, ahora giran alrededor del armario multifuncional y se abren a las bellas vistas sobre el océano Pacífico.

The brilliant white kitchen cabinets, the rectangular tiles and the stainless steel worktops make this small kitchen feel much more spacious.

Die glänzend weißen Küchenschränke, die quer verlegten Kacheln und die Arbeitsfläche aus rostfreiem Stahl sorgen dafür, dass die kleine Küche größer wirkt.

Les placards d'un blanc brillant, les carreaux de faïence oblongs et les plans de travail en acier inoxydable agrandissent visuellement la cuisine.

Los armarios de cocina de color blanco brillante, los azulejos apaisados y las encimeras de acero inoxidable hacen que la pequeña cocina parezca más espaciosa.

CITY VIEW HOUSE

Russian for Fish
www.russianforfish.com
London, UK
753 sq ft (70 m^2)
© Peter Landers

When architects design their own home they become immersed in their job. For Pereen d'Avoine this immersion was absolute: He lived for an entire year in his flat before embarking upon the renovation so that he would get to know its shortcomings... as well as giving him time to gather the funds. Ingenuity is born out of necessity: the renovation cost £30,000 and increased the value of the flat by £80,000. £50,000 worth of ingenuity is not bad!

Beim Entwurf seines eigenen Hauses versenkte sich ein Architekt regelrecht in seiner Arbeit. Für Pereen d'Avoine war das nicht nur ein Sprichwort: Er wohnte ein Jahr lang in der Wohnung, ohne sie umzubauen, um die Mängel zu entdecken... und um Zeit zu haben, die benötigten Gelder aufzutreiben. Not macht erfinderisch: Der Umbau kostete 30.000 Pfund und erhöhte den Wert der Wohnung auf 80.000. 50.000 Pfund Erfindergeist, also. Nicht schlecht!

En concevant sa propre maison, l'architecte a été accaparée par son travail. Pour Pereen d'Avoine, cette immersion fut littérale. Elle passa une année dans l'appartement sans le rénover, pour en découvrir les défauts... et avoir le budget. Le besoin rend ingénieux ; la rénovation a coûté 30 000 livres, alors que la valeur a augmenté de 80 000. Une ingéniosité à 50 000 livres, pas si mal !

Al diseñar su propia casa, un arquitecto se sumerge en su trabajo. Para Pereen d'Avoine, la inmersión fue literal: estuvo todo un año viviendo en el piso sin reformar, con el objeto de ir descubriendo sus carencias... y de tener tiempo para reunir el presupuesto. La necesidad aviva el ingenio: la reforma costó 30.000 libras y aumentó en 80.000 la tasación del piso. 50.000 libras de ingenio, por lo tanto. ¡No está mal!

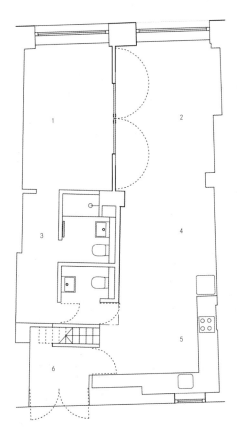

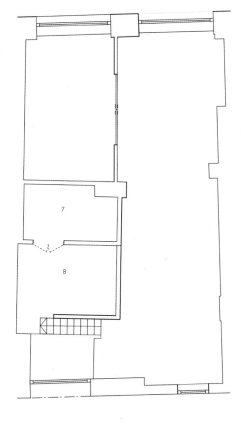

Floor plan

1. Master bedroom
2. Living room
3. Dressing room
4. Dining room
5. Kitchen
6. Lobby
7. Storage room
8. Sleeping
   mezzanine/Study

Mezzanine plan

The original flat was a gloomily renovated former bakery. This is proof that to achieve space and functionality it takes more than just tearing down walls.

Die ursprüngliche Wohnung war ihrerseits ein düsterer Umbau einer alten Brotfabrik. Der Beweis, dass für Raum und Funktionalität etwas mehr als niedergerissene Wände nötig sind.

L'appartement d'origine était une sinistre reconversion d'une ancienne boulangerie. Ce n'est pas qu'en abattant des murs que l'on obtient de l'espace et de la fonctionnalité.

El piso original era a su vez una lóbrega remodelación de una antigua panificadora. La prueba de que espacio y funcionalidad requieren de algo más que de derribar paredes.

Even the knobs were designed by Russian for Fish. Eccentricity defines these architects who call themselves 'The Russian word for *fish*'. All is explained on their website.

Russian for Fish entwarf auch die Türknaufe. Das Exzentrische definiert dieses Studio, das sich schließlich auch ‚Das russische Wort für *Fisch* nennt'. Die Erklärung gibt es auf der Webseite.

Russian for Fish a aussi conçu les pommeaux. Le nom de cette agence excentrique est le « mot russe pour dire *poisson* ». C'est son site web qui l'explique.

Russian for Fish diseñó también los pomos. Lo excéntrico define a este estudio que, al fin y al cabo, se llama 'La palabra rusa para *pez*'. La explicación, en su web.

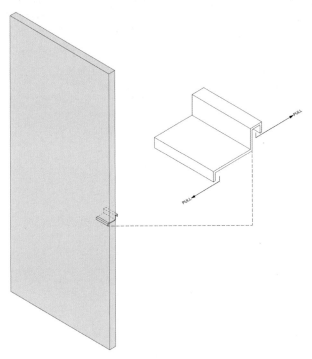

Detail of double pull handle

Speaking of ingenuity: the entire floor is made of wood. The black and white grain is painted on top. The diagonals add width to this over-long house.

Da gerade bereits der Erfindergeist erwähnt wurde: Der gesamte Boden besteht aus Holz. Das schwarz-weiße Muster ist aufgemalt. Durch die diagonalen Quadrate bekommt die in die Länge gezogene Wohnung eine gewisse Breite.

En parlant de génie : tout le sol est en bois. La trame noire et blanche est peinte par-dessus. Les diagonales donnent de la largeur à une maison trop longue.

Hablando de ingenio: todo el suelo es de madera. La trama en blanco y negro está pintada encima. Las diagonales dan algo de anchura a una casa demasiado alargada.

SLAB

k-studio
www.k-studio.gr
Athens, Greece
753 sq ft (70 m²)
© Vangelis Paterakis

This apartment's aesthetic is unmistakeably minimalist, but given its location in the centre of Athens, Greece, at the foot of the steep hill on which the Acropolis stands, *Neoclassical* might be a better word to describe it. The décor elevates this house to elegance. As we have already seen, chic goes beyond the merely functional.

Die Ästhetik dieser Wohnung ist zweifellos minimalistisch. Durch die Lage inmitten von Athen (Griechenland) und am Fuß des steilen Hügels, auf dem sich die Akropolis erhebt, scheint das passende Wort eher *neoklassizistisch* zu sein. Die Dekoration des Hauses steht im Dienst der Eleganz. So erscheint es uns: Der Schick geht über das bloße Funktionelle hinaus.

L'esthétique de cet appartement est résolument minimaliste. Comme il est situé au cœur d'Athènes, en Grèce, au pied de la colline pentue que surplombe l'Acropole, le mot le plus adéquat pour le décrire est *néoclassique*. La décoration de ce logement est au service de l'élégance. C'est ce qu'il nous semblait : le chic va au-delà de la fonction pure.

Sin duda la estética de este apartamento es minimalista, pero ubicado en medio de Atenas, Grecia, como está, y al pie de la empinada colina sobra la que se yergue la Acrópolis, la palabra que parece encajar mejor es *neoclásica*. La decoración de la casa se erige al servicio de la elegancia. Ya nos parecía: lo chic va más allá de lo meramente funcional.

The house is located at the intersection of two streets. Not only does this allow the light to enter, the curvature of the building permeates its design and sets it apart from the rest.

Das Haus liegt an einer Straßenkreuzung. Das setzt nicht nur den direkten Einfall des Lichts voraus: Die kurvige Form des Gebäudes beeinflusst das Design und macht es unverwechselbar.

L'appartement se situe au croisement de deux rues. A part l'accès direct à la lumière, la courbure de l'immeuble imprègne l'architecture et la fait remarquer.

La casa está situada en el cruce entre dos calles. No solo supone el acceso directo a la luz: la curvatura del edificio impregna el diseño y lo distingue.

1. Kitchen
2. Living room
3. Entrance
4. Bedroom
5. Bathroom

Floor plan

THE WHITE APARTMENT

Eva Bradáčová
www.ebarch.cz
Prague, Czech Republic
753 sq ft (70 m²)
© Jiří Ernest

It was the dreams of Eva Bradáčová's clients that really inspired the interior of this home. What they dreamed of was a white interior...and there are many advantages to white. It brings harmony and a sense of cleanliness. It also makes the apartment feel more spacious. It is simple and elegant, and if you get tired of it you can always freshen it up with colourful accessories.

Die Träume der Klienten von Eva Bradáčová waren es, welche die Inspiration für das Innere dieser Wohnung lieferten. Und was sie erträumten, war ein ganz in Weiß gehaltener Innenbereich..., aber das Weiß hat viele Vorteile: Es sieht harmonisch aus und kreiert eine Atmosphäre von Sauberkeit. Die Wohnung wirkt außerdem auch geräumiger. Es ist ganz einfach elegant und wenn man des Weißes müde ist, kann man es immer wieder mit farbigen Accessoires aufpeppen.

L'architecture d'intérieur de cette maison est véritablement nourrie des rêves des clients d'Eva Bradáčová. Ils ont rêvé d'un intérieur blanc... mais le blanc a de nombreux avantages : c'est une couleur harmonieuse, synonyme de propreté. L'appartement semble aussi plus grand. Il est simple et élégant. Si on s'en lasse, on peut toujours le rafraîchir avec des touches de couleur.

Los sueños de los clientes de Eva Bradáčová son lo que realmente inspiraron los interiores de esta vivienda. Y lo que soñaron era un interior blanco..., pero el blanco tiene muchas ventajas: se ve armonioso y crea sensación de limpieza. El apartamento también parece más espacioso. Es simple y elegante y, si te cansas de él, siempre se puede refrescar con complementos de color.

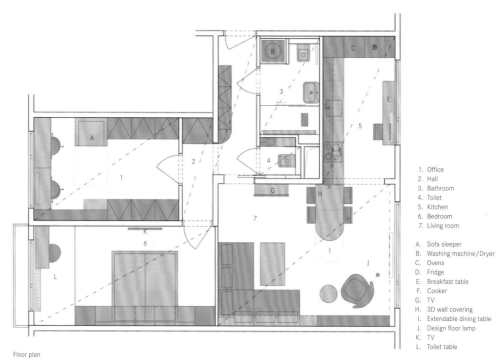

Floor plan

1. Office
2. Hall
3. Bathroom
4. Toilet
5. Kitchen
6. Bedroom
7. Living room

A. Sofa sleeper
B. Washing machine / Dryer
C. Ovens
D. Fridge
E. Breakfast table
F. Cooker
G. TV
H. 3D wall covering
I. Extendable dining table
J. Design floor lamp
K. TV
L. Toilet table

LED lighting strips are used primarily on the ceiling, around the kitchen cabinets and the storage cupboards, and in the hallway.

Die Beleuchtung erfolgt uber LED-Streifen und wird überwiegend an der Decke, um die Küchenmöbel und die Vorratsschränke herum und im Flur verwendet.

L'éclairage à base de rubans LED est principalement utilisé au plafond, autour des meubles de cuisine, des armoires de rangement et dans le couloir.

La iluminación mediante tiras de LED se utiliza principalmente en el techo, alrededor de los muebles de cocina, los armarios de almacenamiento y en el pasillo.

APARTMENT-26D

MODO
www.mo-do.net
Hong Kong, China
775 sq ft (72 m²)
© Rogan Coles

Minimalism (the aesthetics of space and essentials) is like the mathematic result of adding small and chic. Not exactly of course: it is possible to build huge minimalist palaces, or achieve chic by lovingly adding details to a crowded room. But this house is an example of such timely fusion. Minimalism to get something out of the space and fill us with wonder.

Der Minimalismus (die Ästhetik des Geräumigen und des Notwendigen) scheint das mathematische Ergebnis der Summe aus klein und schick zu sein. Hier ist es eindeutig nicht der Fall. Man kann große minimalistische Paläste erschaffen oder durch das genussvolle Anhäufen von Details eine übervolle Wohnung hervorbringen. Dieses Haus jedoch ist ein Beispiel der punktuellen Fusion. Der Minimalismus, um aus dem Raum Nutzen zu ziehen und uns in Staunen zu wiegen.

Le minimalisme (esthétique du spacieux et de l'essentiel) semble l'addition mathématique de ce qui est petit et chic. Cela n'est pas vrai. On peut ériger d'énormes palais minimalistes ou rendre chic une maison bondée de petits détails ravissants. Cette maison est un exemple de cette fusion ponctuelle. Le minimalisme pour mettre l'espace à profit et nous laisser bouche bée.

El minimalismo (la estética de lo espacioso y lo esencial) parece el resultado matemático de sumar pequeño y chic. No es así, claro. Se pueden erigir enormes palacios minimalistas, o lograr lo chic llenando de detalles con encanto una habitación abarrotada. Pero esta casa es ejemplo de esta fusión puntual. El minimalismo para sacarle réditos al espacio, y entumecernos de asombro.

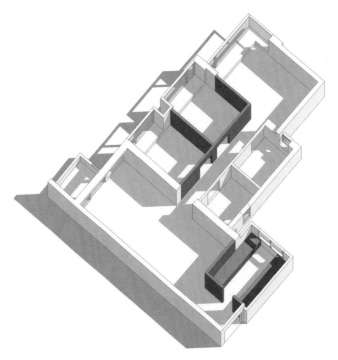

Original axonometry

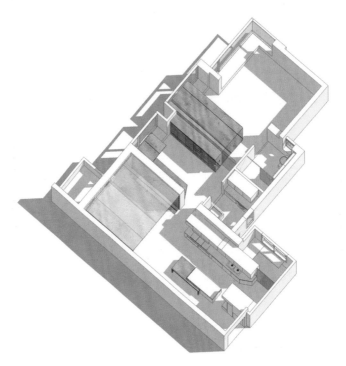

Project axonometry

Floor plan

1. Hall
2. Study
3. Dressing room
4. Master bedroom
5. Dinnig room
6. Kitchen
7. Entrance
8. Pantry
9. Toilet
10. Bathroom

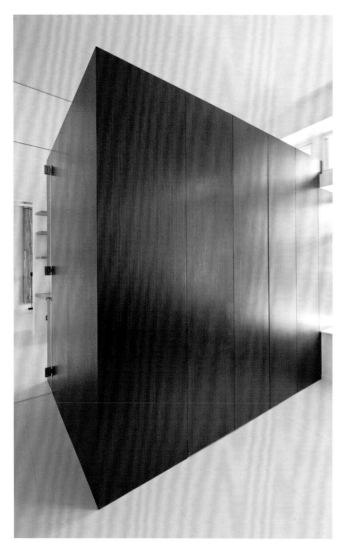

The minimalist aim of clearing each room
works well with small houses: it makes them
bigger. With ingenuity functionality is not
sacrificed for space.

Die minimalistische Absicht jedes Zimmer
recht leer zu halten, ist für kleine Häuser
gut geeignet: Das macht sie größer. Der
Erfindergeist sorgt dafür, dass die Funktionalität
nicht auf Kosten des Raumes geht.

L'intention minimaliste de dégager chaque
chambre va bien aux petites maisons ainsi
agrandies. Avec cette astuce, on a du
fonctionnel sans toucher à l'espace.

La intención minimalista de despejar cada
habitación sienta bien a las casas pequeñas:
las hace grandes. El ingenio consigue que la
funcionalidad no sea a costa de espacio.

APARTMENT IN EL CARMEN

Fran Silvestre Arquitectos
www.fransilvestrearquitectos.com
Valencia, Spain
807 sq ft (75 m²)
© Diego Opazo

This property is located in the El Carmen neighbourhood of Valencia's historic centre, in a three-storey mid-19th century building. With its small surface area and lack of natural light, the renovation project set out to partition off no more than the sleeping areas, leaving the rest open to create a spacious living area with plenty of natural light.

Die Wohnung befindet sich in der Altstadt von Valencia im Viertel El Carmen in einem dreistöckigen Gebäude aus der Mitte des XIX Jahrhunderts. Aufgrund der geringen Grundfläche und dem wenigen natürlichen Licht sah das Projekt vor, einzig und allein die Schlafzimmer zu renovieren, derweil auch ein heller und gut beleuchteter Raum im Wohnbereich geschaffen wurde.

Ce logement est situé dans la vieille ville de Valence, au sein du quartier El Carmen, dans un immeuble à trois niveaux datant du milieu du XIXᵉ siècle. Vu la surface réduite et le peu de lumière naturelle, le projet de rénovation propose de ne compartimenter que les chambres à coucher et crée un espace transparent et bien éclairé dans l'espace de vie commun.

La vivienda se encuentra situada en el casco antiguo de Valencia, en el barrio de El Carmen, en un edificio de tres alturas de mediados del siglo XIX. Con una superficie reducida y escasa luz natural, el proyecto de reforma propone compartimentar únicamente las estancias de noche, mientras crea una espacio diáfano y bien iluminado en la zona de vida común.

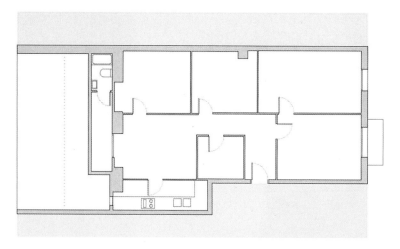

Original floor plan

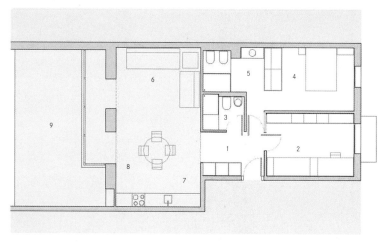

Project floor plan

1. Corridor
2. Bedroom
3. Bathroom
4. Master bedroom
5. Bathroom
6. Living room
7. Kitchen
8. Dining room
9. Terrace

The spacious kitchen-living area makes the most of the ceiling height and connects with the terrace via a huge window that provides plenty of natural light.

Der große Koch-Essbereich nutzt die Höhe der Wohnung komplett aus und vereint sich mit der Terrasse durch eine Fensterfront, durch die viel natürliches Licht hereinkommt.

Le vaste séjour-cuisine profite de la hauteur du logement. Il est relié à la terrasse par une grande baie vitrée qui laisse entrer un flot de lumière naturelle.

La amplia sala de estar-cocina aprovecha al máximo la altura de la vivienda y conecta con la terraza a través de un gran ventanal que aporta abundante luz natural.

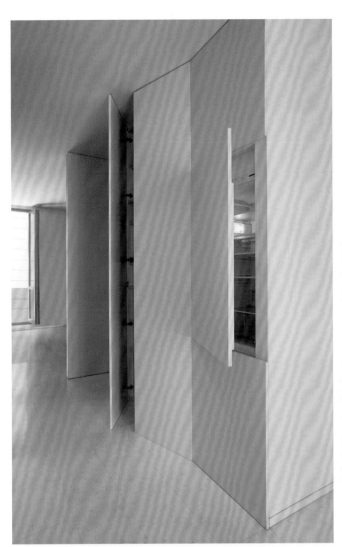

LOFT MM

C.T. Architects
www.cta.be
Bilzen, Belgium
860 sq ft (80 m^2)
© Tim Van de Velde

This house was renovated for the survivor of a car accident. After six months in a coma and three years of rehabilitation he had just learnt to stand again, yet he continues to live with the consequences. With mobility and speech problems, and difficulties in carrying out seemingly the simplest of tasks such as opening a wardrobe, the home needed to adapt to his needs. And he, of course, to it.

Dieses Haus wurde für den Überlebenden eines Autounfalls umgebaut, der nach drei Wochen im Koma und drei Jahren Rehabilitation endlich wieder auf den Beinen stehen konnte. Es blieben jedoch Folgeerscheinungen zurück. Aufgrund der eingeschränkten Mobilität und Problemen beim Sprechen wie auch Schwierigkeiten beim Verrichten der scheinbar einfachsten Dinge (z. B. das Öffnen eines Schranks) musste die Wohnung an ihn angepasst werden. Und vermutlich er sich an sie.

Cette maison a été rénovée pour le survivant d'un accident de voiture. Après trois semaines de coma et trois ans de rééducation, il a pu tenir debout à nouveau. Mais les séquelles restent. Vu ses soucis de mobilité et de langage, ainsi que ses difficultés quant aux choses apparemment simples (comme ouvrir une armoire), le logement a dû s'adapter à lui. Et l'inverse, bien sûr.

Esta casa se reformó para el superviviente de un accidente de coche que, tras seis semanas en coma y tres años de rehabilitación, pudo volver a tenerse en pie. Pero las secuelas permanecen. Con problemas de movilidad y en el habla, y dificultades para las cosas aparentemente más sencillas (como abrir un armario, por ejemplo), la vivienda tuvo que adaptarse a él. Y él, a ella; por supuesto.

Located in a former garage, the house is 30 metres long and just three metres wide. The house is a hallway, with sliding doors, rooms and gadgets grouped around it.

Es befindet sich in einer alten Garage und misst 30 Meter in der Länge, jedoch nur 3 Meter in der Breite. Das Haus ist ein langer Gang: Schiebetüren, Zimmer und verschiedene Mechanismen gruppieren sich um ihn herum.

Cet ancien garage mesure 30 m de long sur 3 m de large. La maison est un couloir, avec des portes coulissantes, des chambres et des mécanismes tout autour.

Situada en un antiguo garaje, mide 30 metros de largo por solo 3 de ancho. La casa es un pasillo: puertas correderas, habitaciones y mecanismos se agrupan a su alrededor.

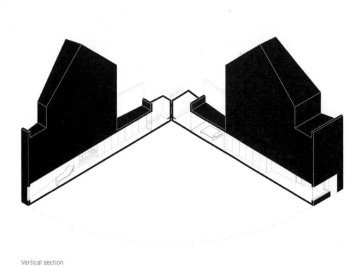

Vertical section

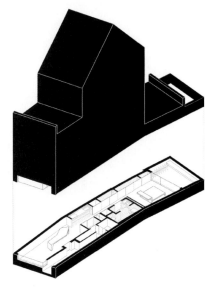

Horizontal section

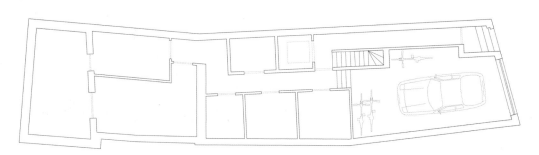

Original floor plan

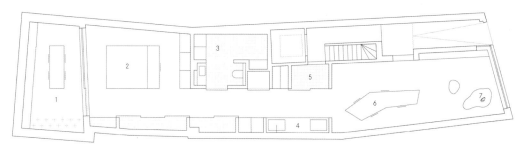

Project floor plan

1. Patio
2. Bedroom/Study
3. Bathroom
4. Kitchen
5. Storage room
6. Dining room
7. Living room

JARDINS APARTMENT

Tavares Duayer Arquitetura
www.tavaresduayer.com.br
São Paulo, Brazil
753 sq ft (70 m²)
© Bruno Cardi © João Duaye

For this renovation the house was stripped to the bone to expose its original structure. The aim was to create the urban, and above all the industrial core that languishes beneath every house. These same lines were then emphasised with the décor. What the house is and what it wants to be are the same: a stylish yet untamed space.

Bei diesem Umbau wurde das Haus kernsaniert, um die ursprüngliche Struktur des Gebäudes wieder zu entdecken. Die Absicht bestand darin, eine urbane und vor allem industrielle Atmosphäre zu erschaffen, die verborgen unter der Verzierung jeder Wohnung schlummert. Später betont dann die Dekoration genau dieselbe Linie. Was das Haus vorgibt zu und was es ist, ist dasselbe: ein eleganter und unbeugsamer Ort.

Lors de la rénovation, la maison a été creusée en profondeur pour faire apparaître la structure d'origine de l'édifice. L'intention était de dévoiler l'ambiance urbaine et surtout industrielle qui se cache, léthargique, sous l'embellissement de tout logement. Ultérieurement, la décoration a renforcé cette idée. La maison est ce qu'elle prétend être, un lieu élégant et indompté.

En esta renovación se excavó en la casa hasta el hueso para sacar a la luz la estructura original del edificio. La intención era lograr la atmósfera urbana y, sobre todo, industrial que subyace aletargada bajo el embellecimiento de cualquier vivienda. Luego, la decoración enfatizó esa misma línea. Lo que la casa es y lo que pretende ser es lo mismo: un lugar elegante e indómito.

Scars are like memories, and when they are chiselled into brick, it seems almost absurd to hide them. The fun is that here they fit with the aesthetic.

Die Narben sind eine Form der Erinnerung und wenn sie in Stein ziseliert sind, erscheint der Versuch, sie verbergen zu wollen, fast absurd. Die Leichtlebigkeit ist es, die hier gut zur Ästhetik passt.

Les cicatrices sont des formes de mémoire. Une fois qu'elles sont marquées dans la brique, les cacher est presque absurde. Elles cadrent bien et de manière frivole avec l'esthétique.

Las cicatrices son formas de memoria y, cuando están cinceladas en ladrillo, ocultarlas casi parece un absurdo. La frivolidad es, además, que aquí encajan con la estética.

Floor plan

1. Living room
2. Bar
3. Kitchen
4. Toilet
5. Laundry
6. Balcony
7. Bedroom

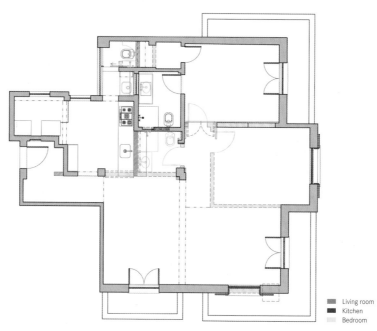

Remodelling plan

Living room
Kitchen
Bedroom

ATTIC RENOVATION IN VERONA

studioWOK
www.studiowok.com
Verona, Italy
860 sq ft (80 m²)
© Federico Villa

Located in a 1960s building, this renovated penthouse was uninhabitable and completely devoid of finishes, electricity and plumbing. The primary objective of its young owner was to create a dynamic space incorporating a bedroom, bathroom and kitchen as well as wardrobe space and a small outdoor area.

Der Eigentümer dieses 250 m² großen Apartments ist ein bekannter Dieser umgebaute Dachboden eines Gebäudes aus dem Jahr 1960 war unbewohnbar und verfügte über kein Finish, keine Elektrizität und Wasseranschlüsse. Bei dem Entwurf stand der Wunsch der jungen Besitzerin im Vordergrund, einen dynamischen Raum mit Schlafzimmer, Bad und Küche zu schaffen wie auch einen Schrankbereich und eine kleine Freiluftzone.

Ces combles rénovés, situés dans un édifice de 1960, étaient inhabitables et ne bénéficiaient pas de finitions, d'électricité ou de point d'eau. Le souhait de sa jeune propriétaire de créer un espace dynamique, avec chambre, salle de bains, cuisine, espace armoire et un petit espace de plein air a été décisif dans le projet architectural final.

Este ático reformado, situado en un edificio de 1960, se encontraba en estado no habitable y completamente desprovisto de acabados, así como de electricidad y de fontanería. En su diseño final primó el deseo de su joven propietaria de crear un espacio dinámico, con un dormitorio, un baño y una cocina, así como un espacio de armario y una pequeña zona al aire libre.

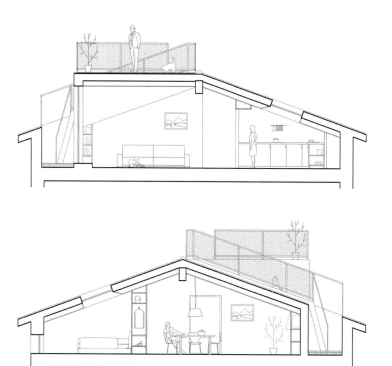

Sections

Floor plan

1. Living room
2. Stairs
3. Dining room
4. Kitchen
5. Corridor
6. Bedroom
7. Dressing room
8. Bathroom

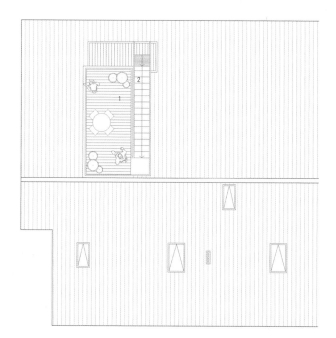

Roof plan

1. Terrace
2. Stairs

In front of the penthouse is a small terrace overlooking the Adige River. From there, a metal staircase provides access to the roof garden.

Gegenüber der Dachluke ist eine kleine Terrasse mit Blick auf die Etsch. Von hier aus gelangt man über eine Metalltreppe hinauf auf das Dach.

Les combles disposent d'une terrasse avec vue sur l'Adige. Elle offre aussi un accès à la toiture via un escalier métallique.

Frente a la buhardilla hay una pequeña terraza con vistas al río Adige. Desde ella, una escalera metálica permite el acceso a la cubierta.

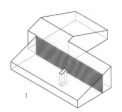

1

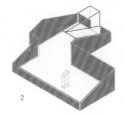

2

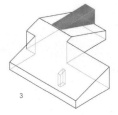

3

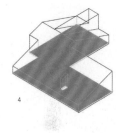

4

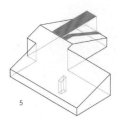

5

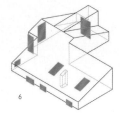

6

7

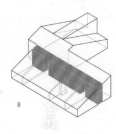

8

Diagrams of construction process

1. Demolition
2. Thermal insulation
3. Dormer
4. Floor
5. Stairs and terrace
6. Windows
7. New roof
8. Custom furniture

FÖHR

Francesco Di Gregorio and Karin Matz
www.francescodigregorio.it, www.karinmatz.se
Föhr, Germany
915 sq ft (85 m²)
© Francesco Di Gregorio

Elevated in the middle of the North Sea, on the small island of Föhr, at the wild mercy of the elements...with frequent storms, persistent fog and downright dangerous tides, the house screams durability. "We did not realise what we had built until we returned the following summer", said Di Gregorio, one of the architects. "Then we saw: a grounded ship."

Inmitten der Nordsee auf der Insel Föhr gelegen und der Gnade einer wilden Natur, zahlreichen Stürmen, dem ewigen Nebel und gefährlichen Strömungen ausgesetzt trägt das Haus seine Härte zur Schau. „Wir waren uns nicht bewusst, was wir da eigentlich gebaut hatten, bis wir im folgenden Frühling zurückkehrten", erklärt Di Gregorio, einer der Architekten. „Dann sahen wir es: Es ist ein in der Erde verankertes Boot."

Cette maison érigée en pleine mer du Nord, sur la petite île de Föhr, à la merci d'une nature sauvage, des tempêtes fréquentes, du brouillard incessant et des marées très dangereuses, exhibe sa dureté. « Nous n'avons pas réalisé ce que l'on avait bâti avant d'y retourner l'été suivant, dit Di Gregorio, l'un des architectes. Nous l'avons alors vu, un bateau échoué sur terre. »

Alzada en medio del mar del Norte, en la pequeña isla de Föhr, y a merced de una naturaleza agreste, con tormentas frecuentes, niebla sempiterna y mareas francamente peligrosas, la casa exhibe su dureza. "No nos dimos cuenta de lo que habíamos construido hasta que volvimos allí al verano siguiente", dice Di Gregorio, uno de los arquitectos. "Entonces lo vimos: es un barco varado en tierra."

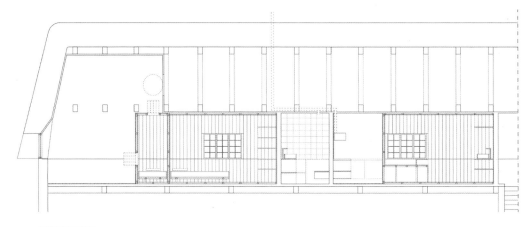

Longitudinal section

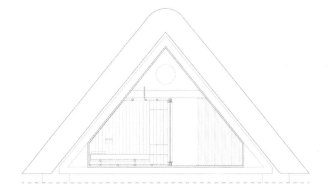

Cross sections

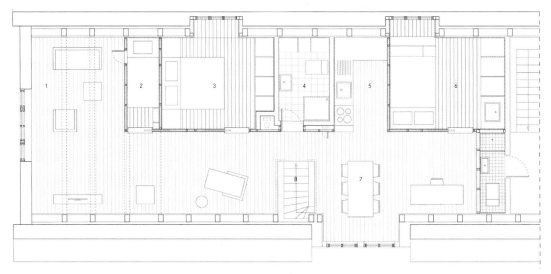

Floor plan

1. Living room
2. Bedroom
3. Bedroom
4. Bathroom
5. Kitchen
6. Bedroom
7. Dining room
8. Stairs

The house is hollow, providing light and space, and interior partitions were done away with wherever possible. The contrast with the island landscape is paradoxical.

Das Haus ist leer, so hat es Luft und Weite: Die Trennwände wurden so weit wie möglich entfernt. Der Kontrast mit der Insellandschaft wirkt beinah paradox.

La maison est creuse, toute en lumière et largeurs. On s'est passé des cloisons intérieures inutiles. Le contraste avec le paysage de l'île frôle le paradoxe.

La casa está hueca, así que es luz y amplitud: se prescindió de las particiones interiores allí donde se pudo. El contraste con el paisaje isleño roza la paradoja.

The hand-crafted Frisian tiles form part of the
island's tradition: they are a sign of prosperity.
If you care to count them you will find there are
exactly 3,500.

Die Fliesen sind von Hand durchbohrt
und friesischen Ursprungs. Ein Teil der
Inseltradition eben: Sie sind ein Zeichen für
Wohlstand. Sie können sie zählen, wenn Sie
wollen. Es müssten genau 3.500 sein.

Les carreaux percés à la main, d'origine
frisonne, sont une tradition de l'île et signe de
prospérité. Comptez-les si vous le voulez. Il y
en a 3 500 pile-poil.

Las baldosas agujereadas a mano, de origen
frisón, forman parte de la tradición de la isla:
son signo de prosperidad. Puede contarlas, si
quiere. Tienen que salirle 3.500 justas.

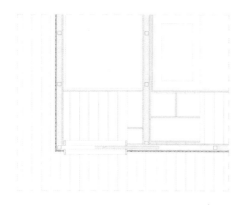

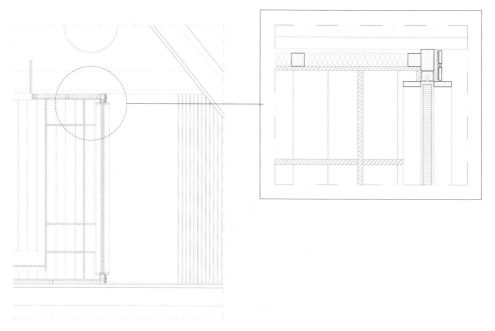

Details of sliding doors

EROSION

Studio NL
www.studionl.com
Athens, Greece
915 sq ft (85 m^2)
© Vassilis Makris

Located on the ground floor behind a lush garden, this apartment was completely gutted for transformation into a very different modern space. The contemporary design uses natural materials (travertine and wood) and bold grey paint, all softened by natural light and contrasted with the LED illumination set.

Diese Erdgeschosswohnung direkt hinter einem Gartenbereich wurde vollständig entkernt, um in einen ganz anderen, modernen Wohnbereich verwandelt zu werden. Das moderne Design beinhaltet natürliche Materialien (Travertin und Holz) und einen verwegenen Grauton, der durch das natürliche Licht gemildert wird, jedoch im Kontrast zum verwendeten LED-Licht steht.

Cet appartement situé en rez-de-chaussée, à l'arrière d'un jardin luxuriant, a été complètement étripé pour être transformé en un espace moderne totalement différent. Le design contemporain a recours à des matériaux naturels (du travertin et du bois) et à une peinture grise osée. Le tout s'adoucit avec la lumière naturelle, en contraste avec le jeu de LED.

Este apartamento ubicado en una planta baja y detrás de un exuberante jardín fue completamente destripado para poder ser transformado en un espacio moderno totalmente diferente. El diseño contemporáneo recurre a materiales naturales (travertino y madera) y a una atrevida pintura gris, todo suavizado por la luz natural y en contraste con el juego de luces LED.

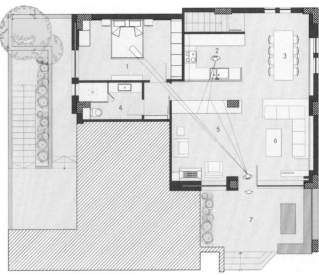

Floor plan

1. Bedrom   5. Study/Hall
2. Kitchen   6. Living room
3. Dining room   7. Veranda
4. Bathroom

The large hanging bookcase with hidden desktop is an "interactive wall" into which all the living spaces of this home are interwoven.

Das große Regal, an dem ein verborgener Schreibtisch hängt, ist eine „interaktive Wand", durch die sich alle Räume der Wohnung miteinander verbinden.

La grande étagère suspendue qui dissimule un bureau est un « mur interactif » à partir duquel s'entremêlent tous les espaces du logement.

La gran estantería colgante con un escritorio oculto es una "pared interactiva" a partir de la cual se entretejen todos los espacios de la vivienda.

SWITCH

Yuko Shibata Office
www.yukoshibata.com
Tokyo, Japan
936 sq ft (87 m²)
© Ryohei Hamada

In a home where the original layout needs to remain untouched, using the idea of a 'switch' to differentiate and separate the different living areas can make a lot of sense. Two large bookcases, each with a large door, allow the same space to be used for different functions, thus switching the house between office and home.

In einer Wohnung, in der die ursprüngliche Aufteilung intakt bleiben soll, erwirbt die Idee des ‚Unterbrechers', der die verschiedenen Lebens- und Arbeitsbereiche von einander trennt, einen neuen Sinn. Zwei große Regale mit jeweils einer großen Tür ermöglichen es durch ihre Wandelbarkeit, die Funktionen innerhalb desselben Raums auszuwechseln. So werden der Wohnraum zum Arbeitszimmer und das Arbeitszimmer zum Wohnzimmer.

Dans un logement où l'étage d'origine doit rester intact, l'idée de l' « interrupteur » comme manière de différencier et de séparer les espaces vie et travail prend tout son sens. En actionnant les deux grandes étagères, chacune munie d'une grande porte, on peut échanger les fonctions à l'intérieur du même espace, adaptant ainsi la maison au bureau et le bureau à la maison.

En una vivienda donde la planta original se ha de mantener intacta, la idea del 'interruptor' como forma de diferenciar y separar las zonas de vida y de trabajo adquiere sentido. Dos grandes estantes, cada uno de ellos con una gran puerta, permiten al accionarse intercambiar las funciones dentro de un mismo espacio, adaptando así la casa a la oficina y la oficina a la casa.

POSITION A

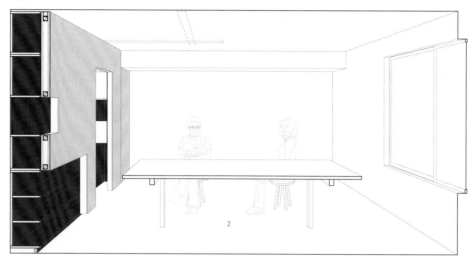

1
2

1. Bookshelf
2. Dining room

POSITION B

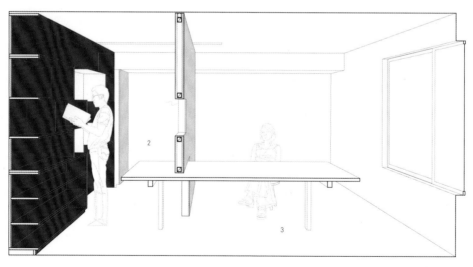

1
2
3

1. Bookshelf
2. Library
3. Meeting room

Detailed section about room transformation:

POSITION A

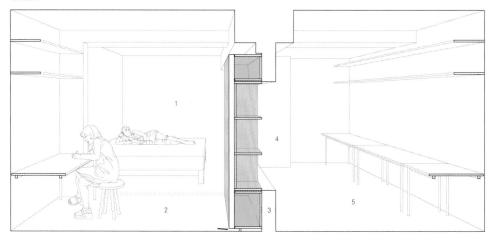

1. Bedroom
2. Study room
3. Bookshelf
4. Bookshelf
5. Working room

POSITION B

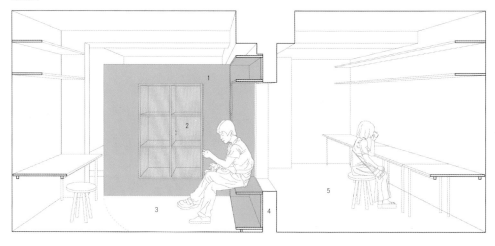

1. Big door
2. Bookshelf
3. Library
4. Bookshelf
5. Working room

Detailed section about room transformation:

When the door is opened it creates a division between the bedroom and the studio, as well as rendering the resulting space a library.

Wenn man die Tür öffnet, wird die Unterteilung von Schlafzimmer und Studio sichtbar. Der so entstandene Raum beherbergt außerdem eine Bibliothek.

Lorsqu'on ouvre la porte, la chambre et le studio se séparent et de plus, l'espace ainsi créé forme une bibliothèque.

Cuando la puerta se abre, se produce la división entre el dormitorio y el estudio y, además, el espacio resultante compone una biblioteca.

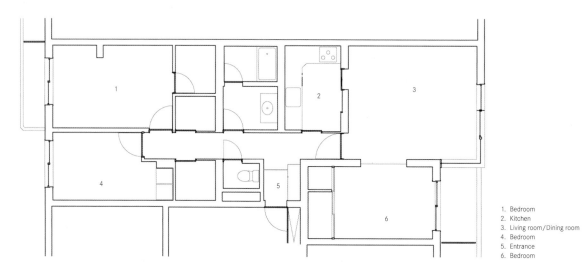

Original floor plan

1. Bedroom
2. Kitchen
3. Living room/Dining room
4. Bedroom
5. Entrance
6. Bedroom

Project floor plan

1. Library/Study
2. Bedroom
3. Closet
4. Closet
5. Bathroom
6. Lavatory
7. Kitchen
8. Library/Dining room
9. Meting room/Dining room
10. Office
11. Laundry
12. Corridor
13. Toilet
14. Entrance
15. Living room
16. Balcony

▨ Office
■ Home

L'APPARTAMENTO DI MARTINA E VALERIO

Spazio 14 10 team: Stella Passerini, Giulia Peruzzi
www.spazio1410.com
Rome, Italy
968 sq ft (90 m²)
© Spazio 14 10: Giulia Peruzzi

The bright colours, the pop-art feel and the recycled objects are the main theme of this home belonging to a young Romanian couple. The living space of the house has been completely redesigned in order to create an informal space with a key focus on recycling and lighting, reflecting the eclectic tastes of its owners.

Die leuchtenden Farben, die Pop-Atmosphäre und die recycelten Objekte sind der Leitfaden dieser Wohnung, die einem jungen römischen Ehepaar gehört. Die Wohnfläche wurde vollkommen neu entworfen, um eine informelle Atmosphäre zu erschaffen, bei der speziellen Wert auf das Recycling und die Beleuchtung gelegt wurde, worin sich der Eklektizismus der Bewohner zeigt.

Les couleurs éclatantes, l'ambiance pop et les objets recyclés sont le fil conducteur de ce logement, propriété d'une jeune couple de Rome. La surface habitable de la maison a été complètement repensée pour créer une ambiance décontractée, où une attention particulière est accordée au recyclage et à l'éclairage, reflet de l'éclectisme des propriétaires.

Los colores brillantes, la atmósfera pop y los objetos reciclados son el hilo conductor de esta vivienda propiedad de una joven pareja romana. La superficie habitable de la casa ha sido completamente rediseñada para crear un ambiente informal en el que se presta especial atención al reciclaje y la iluminación, reflejo del eclecticismo de los propietarios.

The furniture is made from recycled materials such as wine boxes or furniture, and the same goes for the lights. Minimal budget but maximum design aesthetic.

Das Mobiliar wurde aus recycelbaren Materialien, wie zum Beispiel Weinkisten oder recycelten Möbelstücken geschaffen, dasselbe gilt für die Beleuchtung. Unten Budget, oben Design.

Le mobilier se compose de caisses de vins ou de meubles recyclés ; il en est de même pour l'éclairage. Peu de budget, mais beaucoup d'architecture.

El mobiliario está hecho con materiales reciclados, tales como cajas de vino o muebles reciclados; lo mismo respecto a las luces. Bajo presupuesto, alto diseño.

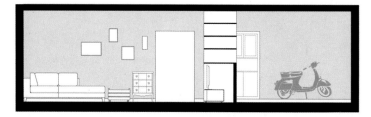

Longitudinal section

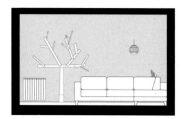

Cross section

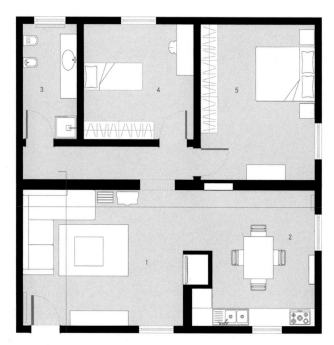

Floor plan

1. Living room
2. Kitchen/Dining room
3. Bathroom
4. Bedroom
5. Master bedroom

The careful blend of bright colours, the decorating of walls with artworks and the unusual design of the lights creates a poetic space that tells a thousand stories.

Die vorsichtige Mischung aus leuchtenden Farben, die Dekoration der Wände mit Illustrationen und der Entwurf der ungewöhnlichen Beleuchtung vereinen sich zu einem poetischen Ort, der Geschichten erzählen kann.

Le mélange soigné de couleurs éclatantes, la décoration illustrée des murs et l'éclairage inhabituel créent un espace plein de poésie, qui raconte une histoire.

La mezcla cuidadosa de colores brillantes, la decoración de muros con ilustraciones y el diseño de luces inusual crea un espacio poético, que cuenta historias.

RHAPSODY IN WHITE

at26
www.at26.sk
Bratislava, Slovakia
990 sq ft (92 m²)
© Ondrej Synak

Here the structure of the roof had to be changed. The loft had been a pigeon house and was falling apart, so several beams needed replacing before the renovation could begin. Thus was born the impossible geometry of the place, and it was only then that the architects realised they needed to find a way of unifying the different shapes of the house. Colour was the answer: white throughout.

Die Struktur des Daches musste verändert werden. Der Dachboden diente als Taubenschlag und war sehr klapprig. Daher mussten vor dem Umbau einige Balken erneuert werden. So entstand die unmögliche Geometrie dieses Ortes. In jenem Moment (und nicht früher) wurde sich das Studio bewusst, dass eine bestimmte Art und Weise her musste, um die verschiedenen Formen des Hauses zu vereinen. Die Antwort fand sich in einer Farbe: Weiß ist hier allgegenwärtig.

La structure de la toiture a dû être changée. Les combles ayant servi de pigeonnier étaient délabrés et des poutres ont été remplacées avant la restructuration. Ainsi est née la géométrie impossible du lieu. C'est à ce moment-là et pas avant que l'agence remarqua qu'il fallait unifier les formes de la maison. La réponse est venue en couleurs, par l'omniprésence du blanc.

Tuvieron que cambiar la estructura del tejado. El ático había servido de palomar y estaba desvencijado, así que, antes de la remodelación, hubo que cambiar algunas vigas. Así nació la geometría imposible del lugar. Fue en ese momento, y no antes, que el estudio se dio cuenta de que necesitaban una forma de unificar las distintas formas de la casa. La respuesta fue un color: la omnipresencia del blanco.

Design sketch

Design sketch

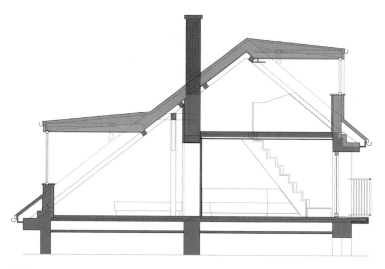

Section

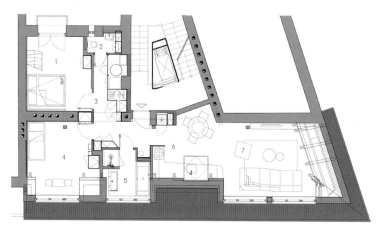

Ground floor plan

1. Master bedroom
2. Toilet
3. Corridor
4. Bedroom
5. Bathroom
6. Kitchen
7. Living room

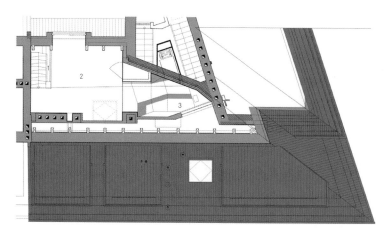

Upper floor plan

1. Stairs
2. Chill out room
3. Double volume

The stairs are cut on a zigzag, like all the lines of this house. Suggestive ideas are found not only in the walls and furnishings, but even in the steps.

Der Schnitt der Treppen wie auch alle Linien dieses Hauses besteht in einem Zickzack-Muster, Die reizvollen Ideen finden sich nicht nur bei den Wänden oder den Möbeln: Oft schreitet man darüber.

L'entaille des escaliers zigzague, comme toutes les lignes. Les idées suggestives sont non seulement sur les murs ou dans les meubles ; on marche souvent dessus.

El corte de las escaleras zigzaguea, como todas las líneas de esta casa. Las ideas sugestivas no se encuentran solo en las paredes o en los muebles: muchas veces, las pisamos.

Upstairs there is an enclosed chill-out area, which in turn overlooks the lounge below.

Im oberen Stockwerk wurde eine Relax-Zone eingebaut, von der aus man das darunterliegende Wohnzimmer gelangt.

Une zone détente est encastrée au niveau supérieur et donne sur le salon en bas.

En el piso superior hay encajonada una zona de relax, que a su vez da al salón de abajo.

REMODELING OF A FLAT IN THE COMTE DE SALVATIERRA STREET

Anna & Eugeni Bach, arquitectes
www.annaeugenibach.com
Barcelona, Spain
1022 sq ft (95 m²)
© Eugeni Bach

It takes work to convert a suite of offices into a home fit for a young family, but it isn't just about pulling down walls. Although the rooms were expanded, their layout remained, with a sub-divided inner section, hallway and open ends. The street-facing playroom was left exactly as it was: the office supplies are now toys.

Der Umbau einiger Büros in eine Wohnung für eine junge Familie klingt nach Arbeit, besteht aber nicht nur in dem Einreißen vieler Wände. Obwohl die Zimmer vergrößert wurden, ist die Aufteilung dieselbe: der unterteilte Innenbereich, der Flur und die beiden lichtdurchfluteten Enden. Man blickt hinaus auf die Straße, das Spielzimmer für die Kinder blieb so, wie es war. Nun gut: Das Büromaterial ist ab sofort Spielzeug.

Transformer des bureaux en un logement pour une jeune famille suppose du travail, mais pas besoin d'abattre trop de cloisons. Les chambres ont été agrandies ; leur distribution a été gardée : intérieur cloisonné, couloir et deux extrémités transparentes. La salle de jeux des enfants, avec vue sur la rue, est restée telle quelle. Les jouets remplaceront les fournitures de bureau.

Convertir unas oficinas en la vivienda de una familia joven supone trabajo, sí, pero no es asunto de derribar muchas paredes. Aunque se ampliaron las habitaciones, se mantuvo su distribución: el interior compartimentado y el pasillo; los dos extremos diáfanos. Encarada a la calle, la sala de juegos para los niños se dejó tal y como estaba. Bueno: el material de oficina serán ahora juguetes.

"Personal belongings and memories," says Anna Bach, "are what makes a space a home and binds you to a place. Architecture is not about pretty photos, it is about living".

„Persönliche Gegenstände, Erinnerungsstücke", sagt Anna Bach, „ist das, was einen Raum wohnlich macht, was einen mit ihm verbindet. Die Architektur ist nicht dazu da, um Fotos zu machen, sondern um darin zu leben."

« Les objets personnels, les souvenirs, dit Anna Bach, font qu'un espace est habité et qu'on s'y attache. L'architecture ne se prend pas en photo, elle se vit. »

"Los objetos personales, los recuerdos", dice Anna Bach, "son lo que hace que se habite un espacio, lo que te liga al lugar. La arquitectura no es para hacerle fotos sino para vivirla."

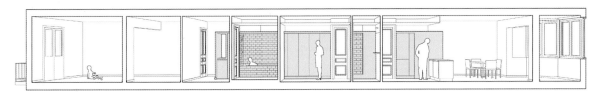

Section

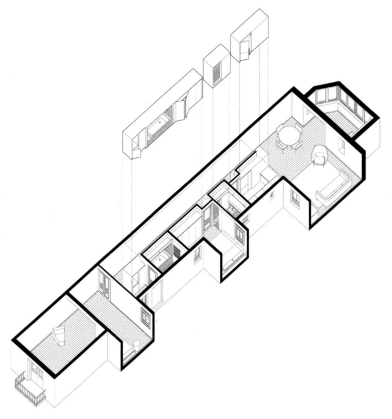

Exploded axonometric view

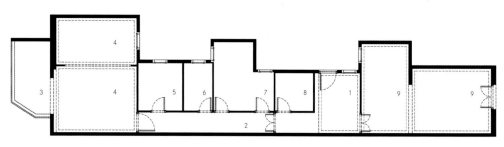

Floor plan

1. Hall
2. Corridor
3. Veranda
4. Living room/
   Dining room
5. Kitchen

6. Main bedroom
7. Main bathroom
8. Bathroom
9. Kids bedroom
10. Playroom

MINIMALIST MOSCOW APARTMENT WITH A BRIGHT AND COZY ATMOSPHERE

ZE|Workroom Studio
www.zeworkroom.com
Moscow, Russia
1076 sq ft (100 m^2)
© Averkina Alexandra, Shibaev Alex and Sevastianova Sima

"A Muscovite minimalist apartment with a bright and friendly atmosphere." The succinct description of this project makes it clear: it is minimalist, but carefully done. The functionality of empty spaces and straight lines can make a house's atmospheric warmth plunge below zero, but not here. The materials chosen and the use of blue serve to retain its warmth. In the intense light of day, sky blue is transformed into a warm colour.

Ein minimalistisches Apartment in Moskau mit einer strahlenden und gemütlichen Atmosphäre. De knappe Beschreibung, mit der sich das Projekt schmückt, lässt keinen Zweifel: minimalistisch ja, aber behutsam. Die Funktionalität der leeren Räume und die geraden Linien verbreiten manchmal in Häusern eine unter Null liegende psychische Temperatur. Hier nicht: Die Materialien und die blaue Farbe geben der Wohnung Wärme. Durch das intensive Tageslicht nimmt der Himmel eine Blaufärbung an.

« Un appartement moscovite minimaliste, pétillant et accueillant. » La brève description du projet est claire : il est minimaliste, mais attention ! Les espaces vides et les lignes droites refroidissent les maisons à des températures au-dessous de zéro, mais pas ici. Les matériaux et le bleu gardent la chaleur. Sous la lumière intense, le bleu clair devient une couleur chaude.

"Un apartamento minimalista moscovita con una brillante y acogedora atmósfera." La sucinta descripción con que se nombró el proyecto lo deja claro: minimalismo sí, pero con cuidado. La funcionalidad de los espacios vacíos y las líneas rectas tienden a enfriar las casas a temperaturas anímicas bajo cero. Aquí no: los materiales y el azul mantienen la calidez del hogar. Bajo la intensa luz del día, el celeste se torna un color cálido.

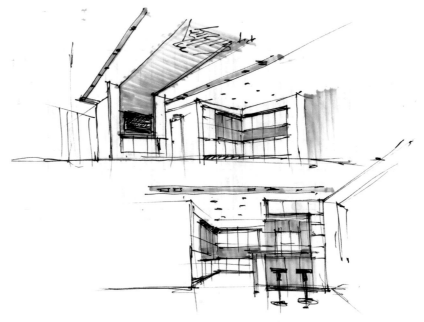

Sketches

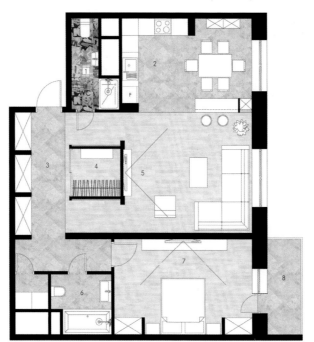

Floor plan

1. Bathroom
2. Kitchen
3. Hall
4. Cloak room
5. Living room
6. Bathroom
7. Bedroom
8. Balcony

The space is a natural polyhedron, creating
the minimalist effect. Any angle that is
not 90 degrees has been banned from the
apartment and curves, too, are a no-no.

Die minimalistischen Züge werden durch die
verwendeten Polieder erzeugt. Jeder klar
herausstechende 90° Winkel ist der Bann des
Apartment. Von den Kurven reden wir gar nicht.

Ce polyèdre a des traits minimalistes. Tout
angle qui n'est pas à 90° a été exclu de
l'appartement. Quant aux courbes, n'en
parlons même pas !

Para rasgos minimalistas, la naturaleza
poliédrica del lugar. Cualquier ángulo distinto
de 90° ha sido proscrito del apartamento. Y
las curvas, ni digamos.

A huge cube in the entrance serves as a closet
and holds the living room TV. This is more
than functionality, it is architecture. It relies on
visual impacts.

Ein großer Würfel im Eingangsbereich dient
als Kleiderschrank und als Stütze für den
Fernseher des Wohnzimmers. Das ist nicht
nur Funktionalität, das ist Architektur. Man
benötigt visuelle Eindrücke.

Dans l'entrée, un énorme cube sert de
dressing et accueille la télé du salon.
L'architecture n'est pas que fonctionnalité. Elle
demande des impacts visuels.

Un enorme cubo en la entrada hace de ropero
y sostiene el televisor del salón. No es solo
funcionalidad, esto de la arquitectura. Se
requieren impactos visuales.

THE STANHILL APARTMENT

Architecture Architecture
www.archarch.com.au
Melbourne, Australia
1076 sq ft (100 m²)
© Tom Ross of Brilliant Creek

Stanhill is a post-war building designed by the famous modernist Frederick Romberg. The apartments are characterised by their open plan format and the abundant natural light that floods in from different sides. Architecture Architecture objective was to create a new design with a minimalist aesthetic on a limited budget.

Stanhill ist ein Gebäude aus der Nachkriegszeit, das von dem berühmten Modernisten Frederick Romberg entworfen wurde. Die Wohnungen zeichnen sich durch die offene Planung der Räume und den ausgezeichneten Lichteinfall, der aus verschiedenen Richtungen möglich ist. Das Ziel von Architecture Architecture bestand in einem neuen Design, obwohl das Budget begrenzt war, und einer minimalistischen Ästhetik.

Stanhill est un édifice d'après-guerre conçu par le célèbre architecte moderniste Frederick Romberg. Les appartements se caractérisent par leur plan ouvert et par l'apport abondant en lumière naturelle qui pénètre par plusieurs côtés. L'objectif d'Architecture Architecture a été de concevoir quelque chose de nouveau, à l'esthétique minimaliste, malgré un budget très serré.

Stanhill es un edificio de la posguerra diseñado por el célebre modernista Frederick Romberg. Los apartamentos se caracterizan por su planificación abierta y por la abundante entrada de luz natural que reciben desde diferentes flancos. El objetivo de Architecture Architecture fue realizar un nuevo diseño, aunque un presupuesto muy ajustado. y una estética minimalista.

A black band of cabinetry runs throughout the entire home. Its purpose is to draw attention to the masterful plan that was designed by the original architect.

Ein schwarzer Streifen aus Ebenholz verläuft durch die gesamte Wohnung. Sein Zweck: Die Aufmerksamkeit auf die großartige Planung des ursprünglichen Architekten zu richten.

Une bande noire en ébène traverse tout le logement, dans le but d'attirer l'attention sur l'organisation spatiale magistrale conçue par l'architecte d'origine.

Una banda negra de ebanistería recorre toda la vivienda. Su propósito: llamar la atención sobre la magistral planificación concebida por el arquitecto original.

Floor plan

1. Dining room
2. Living room
3. Balcony
4. Kitchen
5. Bedroom
6. Bathroom
7. Entrance
8. Bedroom

BERMONDSEY WAREHOUSE LOFT

FORM Design Architecture
www.form-architecture.co.uk
London, UK
1130 sq ft (105 m²)
© Charles Hosea © Mike Neale

The client only requested some minor renovations to adapt this apartment to his needs, but the architects gave him what he really wanted: to knock down the walls so it would resemble an industrial warehouse. As a result it won the "Don't move, Improve!" 2013 interior design prize and the client gained something he hadn't asked for: the apartment of his dreams.

Obwohl der Klient um einige kleinere Änderungen gebeten hatte, um die Wohnung seinen Wünschen anzupassen, entspricht das Studio seinen ganz eigenen Vorstellungen: Die Wände wurden bearbeitet, um die Optik einer Industrie-Lagerhalle zu erreichen. Das Ergebnis gewann 2013 den „Don't Move, Improve!"-Wettbewerb für Innenarchitektur. Und der Klient betrachtet diese Wohnung, die er nicht in Auftrag gegeben hat, als das Apartment seiner Träume.

Le client n'avait demandé que quelques petites modifications pour adapter l'appartement à ses besoins, mais l'agence lui a donné ce qu'il désirait vraiment en supprimant les cloisons pour créer un effet d'entrepôt industriel. En 2013, le projet a remporté le prix d'architecture d'intérieur « Don't Move, Improve ! ». Et le client considère que cet appartement qu'il n'avait pas demandé ainsi est celui de ses rêves.

Aunque el cliente pidió solo algunas reformas menores para adaptar el apartamento a sus necesidades, el estudio dio con sus auténticos deseos: arremeter contra las paredes para lograr un aspecto de almacén industrial. El resultado terminó ganando el "Don't Move, Improve!" de diseño de interiores, en 2013. Y con el cliente considerando esa casa, que él no había pedido, el apartamento de sus sueños.

Although the space is empty, it is also compartmentalised: the lighting and sparse furnishings separate the dining area from the lounge area, the work area and so on.

Obwohl der Raum leer ist, ist er dennoch unterteilt: Die Beleuchtung und das spärliche Mobiliar trennen den Essbereich von dem Bereich zur Entspannung oder dem Arbeitsbereich usw. ab.

Cet espace vide est pourtant cloisonné, car l'éclairage et le peu de meubles présents délimitent les espaces salle à manger, détente, travail etc.

Aunque el espacio sea vacío, también está compartimentado: la iluminación y el escaso mobiliario separan la zona del comedor de la de relax, de la de trabajo, etc.

Sketches

The house has many hidden gadgets. Not
just minimalism and space saving, it has the
glamour of a bat cave or a James Bond movie.

Das Haus genießt es, seinen Mechanismus zu
verbergen. Es ist nicht nur minimalistisch und
spart Platz: Es ist die Freude, der Bathöhle
oder einem der James-Bond-Filme ein bisschen
Glamour entlockt zu haben.

La maison s'amuse en cachant ses
mécanismes. Ce n'est pas que du minimalisme
et du gain d'espace. C'est un glamour sorti de
la Batcave ou des films de James Bond.

La casa disfruta ocultando sus mecanismos.
No solo es minimalismo y ahorro de espacio:
es el gozo de un glamour sacado de la
batcueva, o de las películas de James Bond.

Floor plan by zones

1. Sleep
2. Enter
3. Exercise
4. Grow
5. Eat
6. Relax
7. Work
8. Bathe
9. Dress
10. Wash
11. Cook

PIED-À-TERRE

Baldessari e Baldessari
www.baldessariebaldessari.it
Venice, Italy
1185 sq ft (110 m²)
© Matteo Piazza

Maybe this is what Venice invites. The Baldessari brother architects, use bubbly words to describe their work: a renovation involving the fusion of two 19t century homes (a second floor and a penthouse) in which city and art meet, an ironic counterpoint of baroque and the synthesis of the Venetian spirit. It is easy to be sceptical, but just glance through the window and Venice bursts right in.

Fast scheint es, als würde Venedig selbst dazu auffordern. Die Brüder Baldessari, beide Architekten, wählen blumige Worte, um ihr Werk zu beschreiben: Zwei Wohnungen aus dem XIX Jahrhundert wurden vereint (2. Stock und Dachboden) und der Umbau ist eine Mischung aus Stadt und Kunst, ein ironisches Gegengewicht zum Barockstil und der Synthese der venezianischen Seele. Man kann skeptisch bleiben, sollte aber einen Blick aus dem Fenster werden. Und Venedig erscheint.

Venise y invite, à coup sûr. Les frères Baldessari, architectes, décrivent leur œuvre avec grandiloquence : rénovation de la fusion de deux logements du XIXᵉ siècle (un deuxième étage et des combles), rencontre entre la ville et l'art, contrepoint ironique à son caractère baroque et synthèse de l'âme vénitienne. On peut être sceptique, et puis on regarde par la fenêtre. Et Venise explose.

Será que Venecia invita a ello. Los hermanos Baldessari, arquitectos, eligen palabras espumeantes para explicar su obra: una renovación de la fusión de dos viviendas del XIX (un segundo y un ático) que es intersección entre la ciudad y el arte, contrapunto irónico a su barroquismo y síntesis del ánimo veneciano. Uno puede sentirse escéptico, pero luego mira por la ventana. Y Venecia irrumpe.

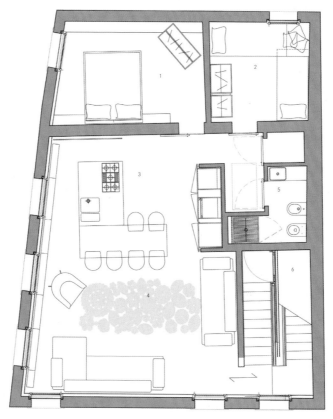

Lower floor plan

1. Master bedroom
2. Bedroom
3. Kitchen
4. Living room
5. Bathroom
6. Stairs

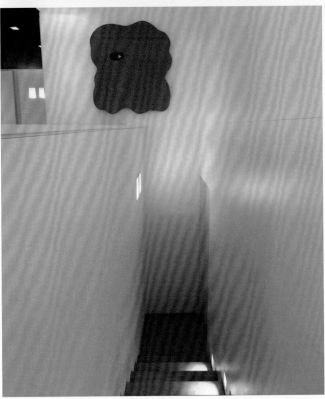

The second floor doubles the size of the penthouse. They are two different boards playing with different rules. One seeks emptiness and space, the other seeks the pleasure of being enclosed.

Der zweite Stock verdoppelt die Größe des Dachbodens. Es handelt sich um zwei unterschiedliche Bereiche, die nach verschiedenen Regeln spielen. Einer sucht Leere und Raum, der andere liebt das Vergnügen, etwas eng zu sein.

Le 2ᵉ niveau double la taille des combles, comme deux damiers n'obéissant pas aux mêmes règles. L'un cherche le vide et l'espace, l'autre à s'encastrer.

El segundo piso dobla el tamaño del ático. Son dos tableros distintos que juegan a reglas distintas. Uno busca el vacío y el espacio; el otro cuida el placer de encajonarse.

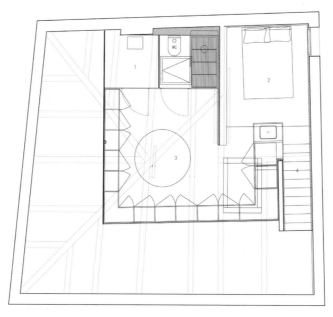

Upper floor plan

1. Bathroom
2. Guest room
3. Living room
4. Stairs

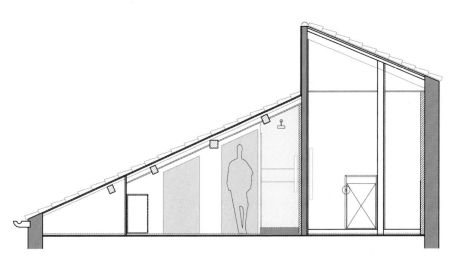

Section of bathroom

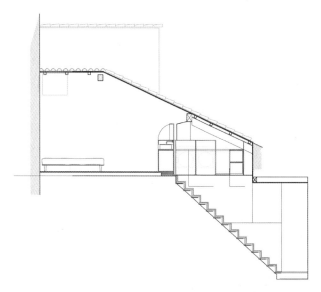

Section of stairs

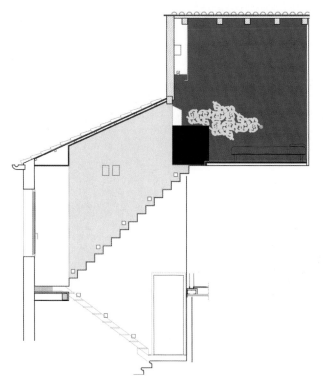

Section of stairs

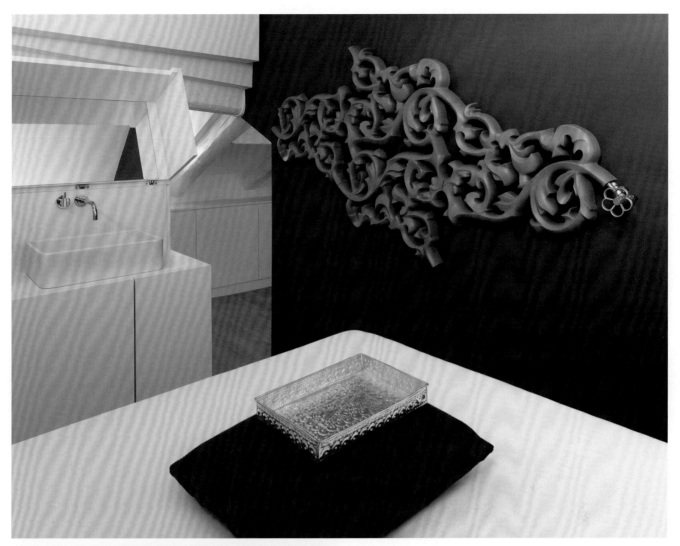

VIA DELLE ORFANE

Con3studio - Elena Belforte & Giusi Rivoira - Architetti Associati
www.con3studio.it
Turin, Italy
1185 sq ft (110 m^2)
© Livio Marrese

"Above all, the apartment is a sensory experience," say the architects. Of this there is no doubt. Within the house, a series of mezzanines breaks the symmetry of the space and makes it playful. Few houses pass their DNA in a single snapshot but this one does: a balcony in the middle of the dining room elevates the eccentric to an autonomous sensory experience.

„Vor allem ist die Wohnung eine sinnliche Erfahrung", sagt das Studio. Und die Bestätigung lässt keinen Zweifel zu: Im Inneren des Hauses durchbrechen ein paar Zwischengeschosse die Regelmäßigkeit des Raums und machen ihn verspielt. Nur wenige Wohnungen vermitteln ihre DNS in einem einzigen Bild. Wie zum Beispiel hier: Ein Balkon inmitten des Wohnzimmers und das Exzentrische wird zur sinnlichen Erfahrung schlechthin.

Selon l'agence, « l'appartement est avant tout une expérience sensorielle ». Pas de place au doute : à l'intérieur, une série de mezzanines cassent la régularité de l'espace, qui batifole. Peu de logements transmettent leur ADN par une seule image. Celui-ci y parvient. Avec un balcon au milieu de la salle à manger, l'excentrique s'érige en expérience sensorielle par excellence.

"Ante todo, el apartamento es una experiencia sensorial", dicen desde el estudio. Y la afirmación no se pone en entredicho: dentro de la casa, una serie de entreplantas rompen la regularidad del espacio y lo vuelven juguetón. Pocas viviendas transmiten su ADN en una sola imagen. Esta lo consigue: un balcón en medio del comedor, y lo excéntrico se eleva a la experiencia sensorial por antonomasia.

It took a lot of work to restore what was left of the original house (the arches date back to the 17th century for example) and achieve the paradox: to make the house feel like nothing ever seen before.

Viel Arbeit war nötig, um das, was vom ursprünglichen Gebäude übrig geblieben war, zu restaurieren (die Bögen aus dem XVII Jahrhundert z. B.) und das folgende Paradox aufstellen zu können: „Das Haus so wahrnehmen, als wäre man nie hier gewesen."

On a travaillé pour restaurer les reliquats de la maison d'origine (comme les arcs du XVIIᵉ siècle) et pour aboutir au paradoxe de « sentir la maison comme quelque chose de jamais vu ».

Se trabajó mucho para restaurar lo que quedaba de la casa original (los arcos del s. XVII, por ejemplo) para lograr la paradoja: "sentir la casa como algo nunca visto antes."

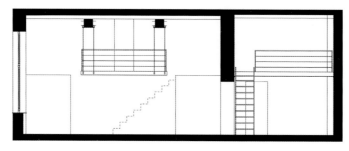

Section a-a

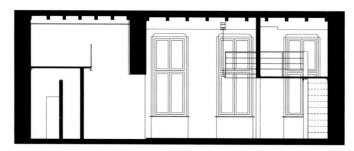

Section b-b

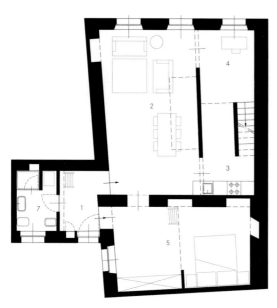

Ground floor plan

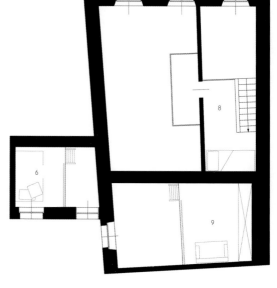

Mezzanine floor plan

1. Entrance
2. Dining room/
   Living room
3. Kitchen
4. Study
5. Bedroom
6. Bedroom
7. Bathroom
8. Bedroom
9. Sitting room

FLAT IN MONTEVERDE

Fabrizio Miccò Architetti Associati
www.fmaa.it
Rome, Italy
1185 sq ft (110 m²)
© Fabrizio Miccò

Harmonised by its use of soft, natural shades, the articulated design of this home's living area creates a series of modules that connect every area of the house. The result is a series of unexpected points of view that end in the reflections and etched transparencies of the vertical partitions.

Der Entwurf für den Innenbereich der Wohnung wirkt durch die Verwendung sanfter, natürlicher Töne harmonisch und entwickelt ein Spiel mit den Räumen, durch das die Verbindung aller Räume dieser Wohnung möglich wird, wodurch wiederum eine Zusammenstellung unerwarteter Gesichtspunkte möglich wird, die zu Spiegelungen und Durchblicken der vertikalen Raumteiler führen.

L'aménagement articulé de l'espace intérieur de ce logement, harmonisé grâce à l'utilisation de nuances naturelles subtiles, déploie un jeu de volumes qui permet de relier toutes les pièces de la maison. Cela offre une combinaison de points de vue inattendus et qui débouchent sur des transparences et des reflets taillés sur les partitions verticales.

El diseño articulado del espacio interior de esta vivienda, armonizado por el uso de suaves tonalidades naturales, desarrolla un juego de volúmenes que permite poner en conexión todas las estancias de la vivienda, lo que propicia una composición de puntos de vista inesperados y que acaban desembocando en reflejos y transparencias talladas en las particiones verticales

Floor plan

1. Terrace
2. Kitchen/Dining room
3. Living room
4. Master bedroom
5. Bathroom
6. Bedroom

GLORIA

hoo
www.hoo-residence.com
Hong Kong, China
1216 sq ft (113 m^2)
© hoo

In this apartment by Hoo, the interpretation of French style is palpable from the very entrance: a kitchen in the purest vintage style, classic walnut hardwood floors, an elegant marble fireplace, designer lamps etc, all of which are highlighted against decorative accessories from around the world and designer furniture pieces by Hoo.

Die vom französischen Stil inspirierte Interpretation dieser Wohnung durch Hoo macht sich direkt im Eingangsbereich bemerkbar: eine Küche in reinem *Vintage*-Stil, Holzböden aus klassischem Nussbaum, ein eleganter Kamin aus Marmor, Designer-Lampen... Betont wird dies alles durch Dekor-Elemente aus allen Ländern der Erde und Design-Möbeln von Hoo.

Dans cet appartement, l'interprétation du style français par Hoo est visible dès l'entrée : une cuisine dans le plus pur style vintage, des sols en bois de noyer classique, une élégante cheminée en marbre, des lampes design... Tout ceci renforcé par des accessoires de décoration du monde entier et des meubles design signés Hoo.

La interpretación del estilo francés en este apartamento por parte de Hoo es palpable desde la mismísima entrada: una cocina al más puro estilo *vintage*, suelos de madera de nogal clásico, una elegante chimenea de mármol, lámparas de diseño... Acentuado todo ello con accesorios de decoración de todo el mundo y muebles de diseño de Hoo.

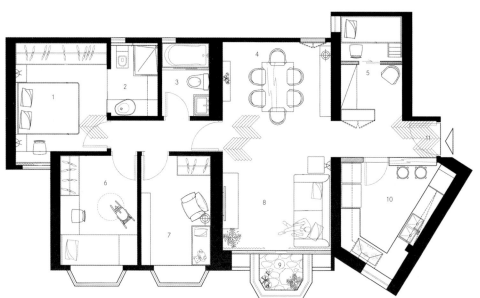

Floor plan

1. Master bedroom
2. Bathroom
3. Bathroom
4. Dining room
5. Storage room/
   Cloak room
6. Bedroom
7. Bedroom
8. Living room
9. Balcony
10. Kitchen
11. Entrance

The reconstruction of the original kitchen in the new open kitchen space allows for natural light to flow in as far as the entrance.

Die Rekonstruktion der ursprünglichen Küche in der aktuellen, offenen Küche ermöglicht es, das natürliche Licht auszunutzen, das durch den Eingangsbereich hereinfällt.

La transformation de la cuisine d'origine en cuisine ouverte permet de profiter de la lumière naturelle, qui finit par envahir l'entrée.

La reconstrucción de la cocina original en la actual cocina abierta permite el aprovechamiento de la luz natural, que acaba inundando la entrada.

EAST LONDON APARTMENT

Draisci Studio
www.draisci.com
London, UK
1290 sq ft (120 m^2)
© Morten Odding

"For reasons as yet unclear", say Draisci architects, "the kitchen was previously situated in a corner of one of the ground floor bedrooms". Complicated indeed! This renovation is a happy and colourful celebration of a new start: a fully equipped kitchen in a house that desperately needed it. The lounge takes on this new function without being overshadowed. It's all about placement.

„Aus Gründen, die es noch zu klären gibt", sagt das Draisci Studio, „befand sich die Küche vorher in einer Ecke eines der Schlafzimmer der Wohnung im unteren Stock." Zumindest eine heikle Situation! Dieser Umbau ist eine fröhliche und bunte Feier einer Vereinigung: Eine vollständig ausgestattete Küche in einer Wohnung, der es daran fehlte. Das Wohnzimmer hat die neue Funktion angenommen, ohne dass es düsterer wurde. Alles eine Frage der Zustimmung.

« Pour des raisons encore à éclaircir, la cuisine était dans un coin de l'une des chambres de l'étage d'en bas », dit-on chez Draisci Studio. Quelle drôle d'affaire! Cette rénovation est la célébration joyeuse et colorée d'un rattachement, celui d'une cuisine toute équipée dans une maison qui en manquait. Le salon accueille pleinement cette nouvelle fonction sans s'assombrir.

"Por motivos aún por esclarecer", dicen desde Draisci Studio, "la cocina se encontraba antes en un rincón de uno de los dormitorios del piso de abajo". ¡Menuda situación comprometida! Esta reforma no es la celebración alegre y colorida de una incorporación: una cocina completamente equipada en una casa que carecía de ella. El salón recibe la nueva función sin oscurecerse. Es todo acogimiento.

The kitchen matches with the motley decoration of the lounge. The colours are inspired by the world of food: tomatoes, lemons, curry, saffron and red wine.

Das Aussehen der Küche passt zur bunten Dekoration des Wohnzimmers. Die Inspiration für die Farben waren Lebensmittel aus aller Herrn Länder: Tomaten, Zitronen, Curry, Safran und Rotwein.

La cuisine cadre avec la décoration bigarrée du salon. Les couleurs s'inspirent de la nourriture du monde : tomates, citrons, curry, safran et vin rouge.

El aspecto de la cocina encaja con la decoración variopinta del salón. Los colores se inspiran en la comida por el mundo: tomates, limones, curry, azafrán y vino tinto.

South façade

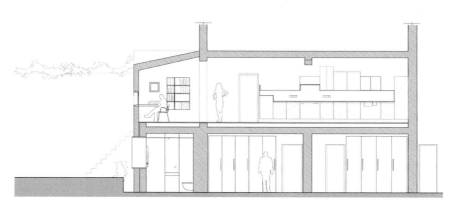

Section b-b

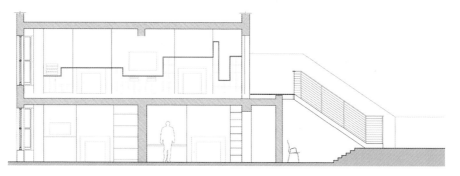

Section c-c

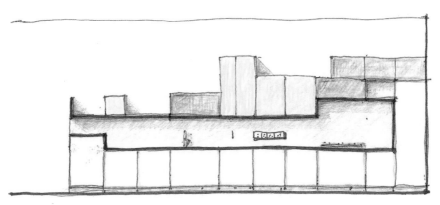

Sketch

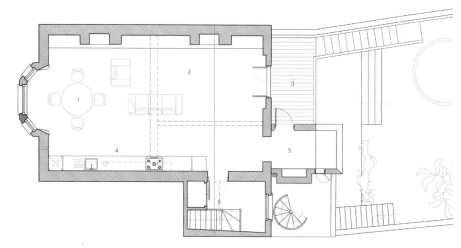

First floor plan

1. Dining room
2. Living room
3. Roof terrace
4. Kitchen
5. Study
6. Stairs

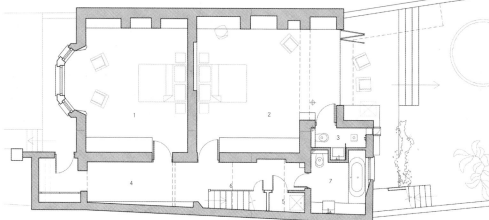

Ground floor plan

1. Bedroom
2. Bedroom
3. Bathroom
4. Entrance
5. Laundry
6. Stairs
7. Bathroom

PADDINGTON TERRACE HOUSE

Danny Broe Architect
www.dannybroearchitect.com
Paddington, Australia
1290 sq ft (120 m²)
© Karina Illovska

When renovating the ground floor of this home, the owners' wishes were
a key consideration: to make a connection with the garden and to give a
contemporary twist to the kitchen and new living spaces. Thus the new kitchen
is a centrepiece around which the entire design revolves, unifying it with the
living areas and dining room, which in turn open out to the garden.

Bei der Renovierung des unteren Stockwerks dieses Hauses wurden die
Wünsche der Besitzer berücksichtigt: Eine Verbindung mit dem Garten und der
Küche und den neuen Zimmern ein zeitgenössisches Flair verleihen. Auf diese
Weise wurde die Küche zum Zentrum, um das herum der Rest des Entwurfs
angeordnet wurde, d.h. der Wohn- und der Essbereich, die ihrerseits auf den
Garten hinausgehen.

La rénovation du niveau inférieur de ce logement a tenu compte du souhait
des propriétaires, celui de créer un lien avec le jardin et donner une touche
contemporaine à la cuisine et aux nouveaux espaces de vie. Ainsi, la nouvelle
cuisine est le centre du nouveau projet architectural. Elle rassemble autour
d'elle les espaces séjour et salle à manger, ouverts sur le jardin.

En la renovación del nivel inferior de esta vivienda se tuvo en cuenta la voluntad
de los propietarios: conectar con el jardín y dotar a la cocina y a los nuevos
espacios de vida de un toque contemporáneo. De este modo, la nueva cocina
es el centro en torno al cual girará todo el diseño al unificarse a su alrededor las
zonas de estar y comedor, que se abren al jardín.

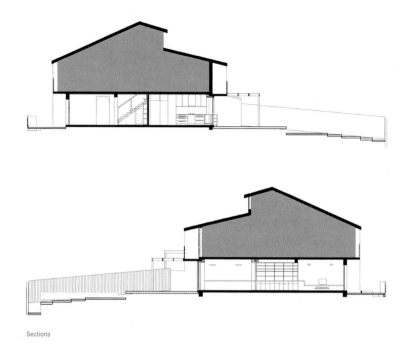

Sections

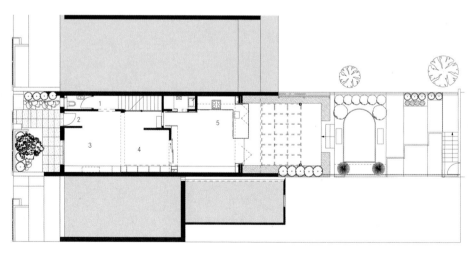

Ground floor plan

1. Toilet
2. Entrance
3. Living room
4. Reading area
5. Kitchen

A long wooden bench runs the entire length of the house, evolving from stylish kitchen worktop to spacious library area with bookshelves.

Eine große Holzbank verläuft entlang der gesamten Länge des Hauses und verwandelt sich von einem eleganten Küchenregal in eine ausgedehnte Bibliothek mit Regalen.

Un long banc en bois traverse toute la maison sur toute sa longueur. Cet élégant comptoir de cuisine devient ainsi une grande bibliothèque munie d'étagères.

Un largo banco de madera recorre toda la longitud de la casa, transformándose de un elegante estante de cocina a una amplia biblioteca con estanterías.

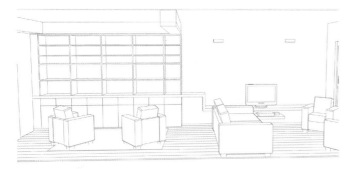

Sketch of TV area

Sketch of the kitchen

The kitchen is integrated in the living space
and open to the exterior. It is more than just a
functional living area, it is a place in which to
meet and celebrate.

Die offene Küche, die in den Wohnbereich
integriert ist, stellt nicht einfach nur einen
funktionellen Bereich dar. Es ist ein Ort, an
dem man ankommt und an dem man feiert.

Insérée dans l'espace de vie et ouverte sur
l'extérieur, la cuisine n'est pas qu'une zone
fonctionnelle ; c'est un lieu d'arrivée où l'on
fait la fête.

La cocina, integrada en el espacio de vida y
abierta al exterior, no es meramente una zona
funcional: es un lugar de llegada y celebración.

CASA CAMACHINHOS

Studio ARTE
www.studioarte.info
Lagos, Portugal
1345 sq ft (125 m^2)
© Luis da Cruz

This renovation involved the conversion of an old property into a complete apartment, which shares its rear with the gardens of the Palace of Lagos. The design is an effective mishmash of comfort and simplicity, with a minimalist design perspective and subtle notes of baroque and Arabian mysticism.

Diese Renovierung schloss die Umwandlung einer alten Wohnung in ein komplettes Apartment mit ein, das sich die Rückseite mit den Gärten des Schwimmbads des Palacio de Lagos teilt. Das Design ist eine effektive Mischung aus Komfort und Schlichtheit, die Dekoration ist minimalistisch und man bemerkt subtile Noten des barocken und arabischen Mystizismus.

Cette rénovation a supposé la transformation d'un ancien logement en un appartement entier, dont la partie arrière est partagée avec les jardins de la piscine du Palais de Lagos. Son architecture est un méli-mélo effectif de confort et de simplicité, avec une décoration à la perspective minimaliste et des notes subtiles de mysticisme baroque et arabe.

Esta renovación supuso la conversión de una antigua vivienda en un completo apartamento, el cual, además, comparte la parte trasera con los jardines de la piscina del Palacio de Lagos. Su diseño es una mezcolanza efectiva de comodidad y simplicidad, con una decoración de perspectiva minimalista y sutiles notas de misticismo barroco y árabe.

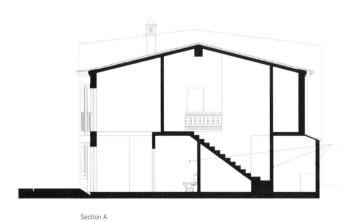

Section A

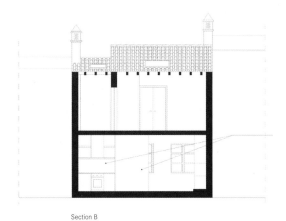

Section B

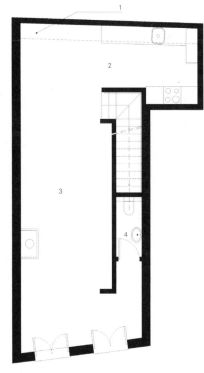

Ground floor plan

1. Fanlight window area
2. Kitchen
3. Living room
4. Toilet

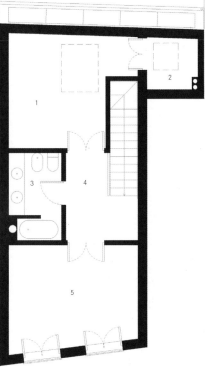

First floor plan

1. Bedroom
2. Dressing room
3. Bathroom
4. Hall
5. Bedroom

The use of the traditional Portuguese *calçada*
polished stone on the ground floor is a tribute
to Portuguese culture in a modern, minimalism
setting.

Die Dielen des unteren Stockwerks wurde
mit dem typisch portugiesischen *Calçada*-
Schliff versehen: Eine Hommage an die
lusitanische Kultur inmitten einer modernen
und minimalistischen Umgebung.

La pierre polie portugaise *(calçada)* utilisée
en carrelage pour le bas est un hommage à
la culture lusitanienne dans une ambiance
moderne et minimaliste.

El pavimento de la planta baja, realizado con
la típica *calçada* pulida portuguesa, es un
homenaje a la cultura lusitana en un entorno
moderno y minimalista.

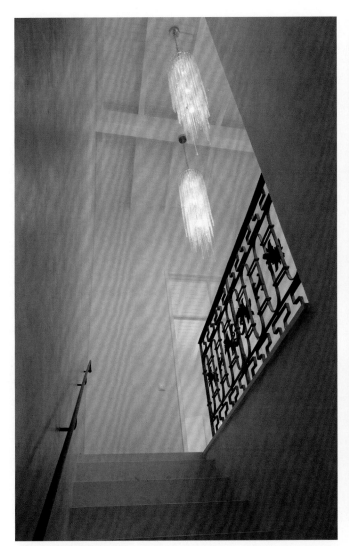

BLACK HOUSE

Andrew Maynard Architects
www.maynardarchitects.com
Melbourne, Australia
1442 sq ft (134 m^2)
© Peter Bennets

Located in an old MacRobertson factory, this apartment required renovation in order to adapt for the birth of the owners' son. What was previously the perfect apartment for a young couple has now been transformed into a place in which every space is adapted to the new needs and functions of the family.

Der Umbau dieser Wohnung, die sich in einer alten MacRobertson-Fabrik befindet, begann mit dem Vorhaben, sie für die Geburt der Kinder der Besitzer vorzubereiten. Was vorher die perfekte Wohnung für ein junges Paar war, verwandelte sich nun in einen Ort, an den alle Räume an die Bedürfnisse und Gewohnheiten einer Familie angepasst wurden.

Situé dans une ancienne usine MacRobertson, cet appartement a dû être rénové afin de l'adapter à la naissance du fils des propriétaires. Auparavant parfait pour un jeune couple, c'est maintenant un lieu où tous les espaces s'adaptent aux nouveaux usages et habitudes de la famille.

La reforma de este apartamento situado en una antigua fábrica MacRobertson se pone en marcha ante la necesidad de adaptar la vivienda al nacimiento del hijo de los propietarios. Lo que antes era el apartamento perfecto para una pareja de jóvenes adultos, se transforma ahora en un lugar donde todos los espacios se adaptan a la nuevos usos y hábitos de la familia.

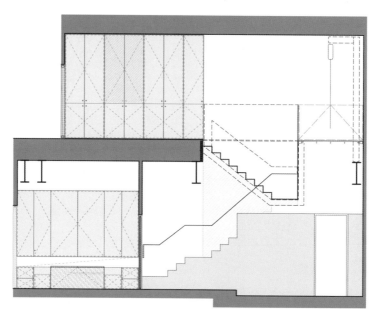

Section

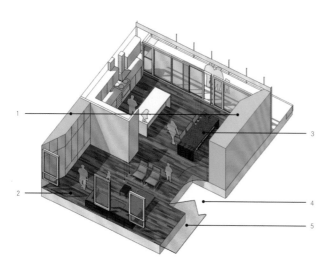

Upper level axonometry

1. Storage: full height storage is kept along the wall to keep the space open and clear
2. Living space: moved to this location because this area is darker which is more suited for a tv room
3. Dining: moved to the old living room, which gives the dining room better connection with the kitchen and the balcony
4. Spiral stair
5. Mesh flooring, hinged to allow furniture to move up

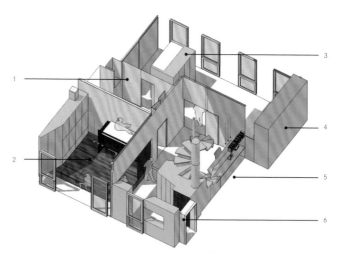

Lower level axonometry

1. Bathroom
2. Bedroom: plinth which acts toy box and floor
3. Joinery to master bedroom addition joinery added to the existing
4. Full height joinery which doubles as bed head
5. Open study
6. Entry joinery

The staircase is crucial in the design: it is at once a desk, a laundry and a piece of furniture. It enables the light to be shared between the two levels and is a playground for the children.

Die Treppe ist der Mittelpunkt des Entwurfs: Sie ist Schreibtisch, Waschraum und Möbelstück; sie ermöglicht es, das Licht auf die beiden Stockwerke aufzuteilen und sie ist der Spielplatz für die Kinder.

L'escalier est essentiel, car il joue le rôle de bureau, buanderie et meuble ; il distribue la lumière sur deux étages et crée un espace jeux pour les enfants.

La escalera es capital en el diseño: es escritorio, lavandería y mueble; permite compartir la luz entre los dos niveles; y es zona de juegos para los niños.

THE LIFE OF A
PARENT.....

PICKING THINGS UP
OFF THE FLOOR.

THE LIFE OF A
PARENT.....

PICKING THINGS UP
OFF THE FLOOR.

ENTROPY + DECAY OF A
TIDY HOUSE. THIS
IS THE ONLY CONSTANT
IN A HOUSE WITH CHILD.

USE GRAVITY! MAKE THE CHILD
PICK IT UP.

SWEEP
LID

NEW
FLOOR

TOY
BOX
BETWEEN

EXTG
FLOOR

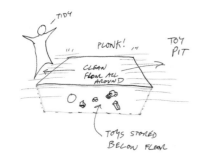

TIDY

PLONK! "

TOY
PIT

CLEAN
FLOOR ALL
AROUND

TOYS STORED
BELOW FLOOR

CLEANING
UP IS FUN!

FLOOR
AS
TOY BOX

(LET GRAVITY
DO THE WORK)

COLOURFUL
RUBBER

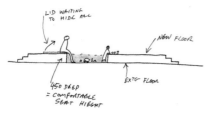

LID WAITING
TO HIDE ALL

NEW FLOOR

EXTG FLOOR

450 DEEP
= COMFORTABLE
SEAT HIEGHT

Sketches of floor as toy box

SIMPLY SHOVE
TO TIDY.

Sketches of floor as toy box

446

The floor is like a giant toy box. This is the original solution that was dreamt up by Andrew Maynard to ensure that gravity would not conspire against the children.

Der Boden ist eine große Kiste voller Spielzeug. Dabei handelt es sich um die originelle Lösung von Andrew Maynard, um zu verhindern, dass die Schwerkraft sich gegen die Kinder verschwört.

Le sol est une grande caisse à jouets. C'est la solution originale trouvée par Andrew Maynard, pour éviter que lorsque les enfants jettent leurs jouets par terre, cela ne se retourne contre eux. Plus d'énervement, les jouets seront rangés !

El suelo es una gran caja de juguetes. Esta es la original solución que Andrew Maynard encuentra para evitar que la gravedad conspire contra los niños.

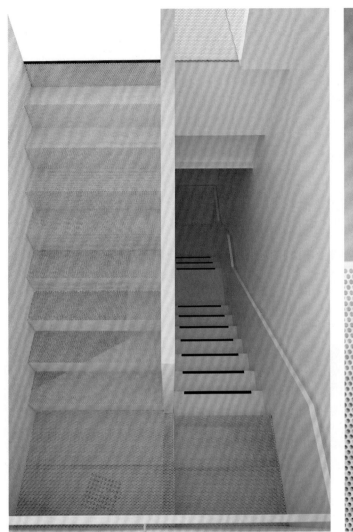

451

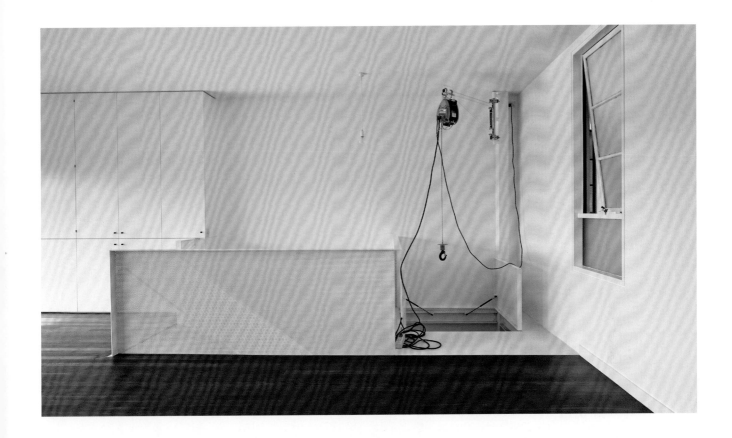

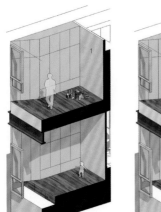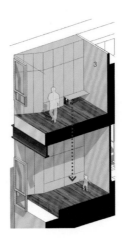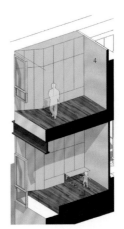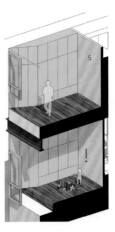

Diagram of floor as toy box

1. Toys on the floor in the living room
2. Joinery flips open, to reveal vertical toy chute
3. Sweep toys into the chute
4. Toys fall through the joinery and back into the bedroom downstairs
5. Play!

RESTORATION OF A HOUSE-YARD IN GRACIA

Carles Enrich
www.carlesenrich.com
Barcelona, Spain
1560 sq ft (145 m²)
© Enric Fabre © Carles Enrich

This wild renovation of an old dry cleaner's with adjoining courtyard took an empty space and transformed it into something desirable. The result is a house full of light. There are no walls, no stairs fixed into the ground, and nothing screwed too tightly down. It is a stimulating house, and so it should be, with a bedroom hanging over the workspace!

Dieser ungestüme Umbau einer alten Reinigung neben einem Innenhof bestand in der Übernahme eines Luftraums, der nach Belieben renoviert wurde. Das Ergebnis ist ein großzügiges Haus. Es gibt keine Wände, noch sind Treppen im Boden verankert: Nichts ist mit ihm fest verschraubt. Ein stimulierendes Haus. Das sollte es auch sein, schließlich arbeitet man hier, während das Schlafzimmer über einem schwebt.

Cette restructuration sauvage d'une ancienne teinturerie et de sa cour s'empare de l'espace vide pour le transformer avantageusement. Il en résulte une maison légère, bien sûr. Il n'y a pas de murs, pas d'escaliers ancrés dans le sol ; rien n'y est vraiment défini. Une maison stimulante. Comme doit l'être le fait d'avoir sa chambre surplomber son bureau.

Esta remodelación salvaje de una antigua tintorería junto a un patio supuso coger un volumen de aire dado y modelarlo a voluntad. El resultado, por supuesto, es una casa liviana. No hay paredes, ni escaleras esculpidas en el suelo: nada se atornilla con demasiada fuerza a él. Una casa estimulante. También debe serlo, al fin y al cabo, trabajar con el dormitorio pendiendo encima de tu cabeza.

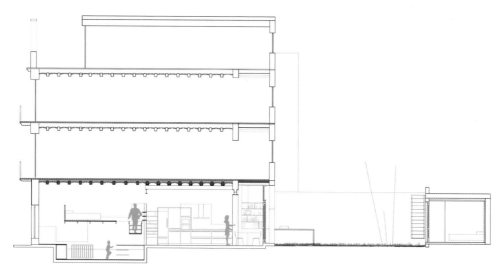

Longitudinal section

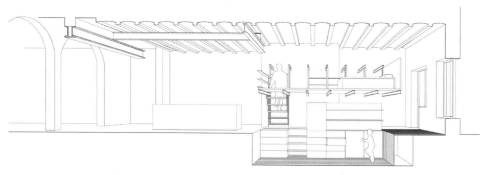

Longitudinal section of bedrooms in two levels

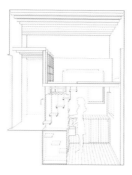

Cross section of bedrooms in two levels

The courtyard is a like a slice of fresh air
that has been conquered outside. For most
of the year it serves the house as an extra
bedroom. Its trees represent nature grafted
into the cityscape.

Der Innenhof ist ein Stück Raum unter freiem
Himmel, der dem Außenbereich abgetrotzt
wurde: Fast während des gesamten Jahres
dient er als weiterer Raum des Hauses. Die
Bäume dort sind ein Stück Natur inmitten
der Stadt.

La cour, un morceau d'air conquis sur
l'extérieur, sert de pièce supplémentaire
durant presque toute l'année. Grâce à ses
arbres, la nature se greffe à la ville.

El patio es un pedazo de aire libre conquistado
al exterior: durante casi todo el año sirve como
una habitación más de la casa. Sus árboles son
naturaleza injertada en la ciudad.

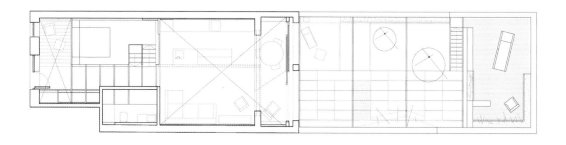

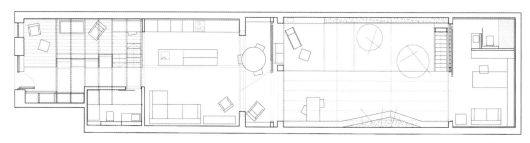

Plans

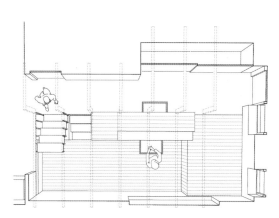

Plan of lower level

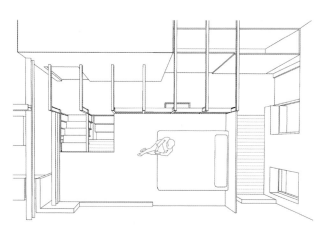

Plan of upper level

Thanks to the lack of interior walls and open structure, the light from the courtyard fills every corner of the house. This is the *'raison d'être'* of the house's shape.

Dank des Fehlens der Innenwände und der offenen Struktur beleuchtet das Licht von außen jeden Winkel des Hauses. Das ist die *raison d'être* für die Gestalt des Raumes.

Vu l'absence des cloisons et sa structure ouverte, la lumière de la cour arrive dans tous les coins de la maison. C'est la raison d'être de la forme de ce lieu.

Gracias a la ausencia de paredes interiores y a su estructura abierta, la luz del patio alcanza cada rincón de la casa. Esa es la *raison d'être* de la forma del lugar.

HOME 07

i29 I Interior Architects
www.i29.nl
Amsterdam, Netherlands
1615 sq ft (150 m²)
© i29 I Interior Architects

A lot of walls were knocked down during the renovation of this two-floor apartment in order to create a large, open home for a family of four. A layer of white spray paint was then applied onto this 'canvas' along with the curious bubble effect created from laser-cut holes. For sure, even in a vacuum it is possible to make your personality stand out.

Bei der Renovierung dieser zweistöckigen Wohnung wurden zahlreiche Wände eingerissen, um einen ausgedehnte und lichtdurchfluteten Ort für eine vierköpfige Familie zu schaffen. Auf einer Leinwand wurde eine weiße Farbschicht aufgesprüht und dann dieser frische Locheffekt mit Hilfe des Laserstrahls erzeugt. Hier ist der Beweis: Auch der leere Raum verfügt über seine eigene Persönlichkeit.

Plusieurs cloisons ont été démolies lors de la rénovation de ce duplex, afin d'offrir un foyer ample et transparent à cette famille de quatre membres. On a appliqué sur cette « toile » une couche de peinture blanche en bombe, et cela s'ajoute à l'effet pétillant et très curieux des trous coupés au laser. Il faut se rendre à l'évidence : même le vide peut exhiber sa personnalité.

En la reforma de este apartamento de dos pisos, se echaron multitud de paredes abajo para ofrecer un hogar amplio y diáfano a una familia de cuatro miembros. Sobre este lienzo, se aplicó la capa de pintura blanca en espray y el curiosísimo efecto burbujeante de los agujeros cortados a láser. Hay que rendirse a la evidencia: incluso el vacío puede lucir su propia personalidad.

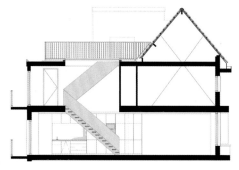

Longitudinal section

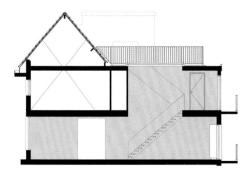

Longitudinal section

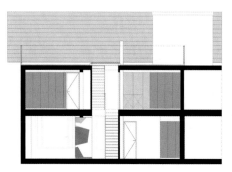

Cross section

First floor

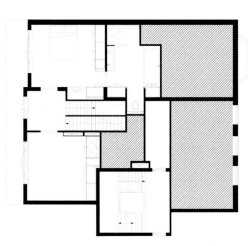

Second floor

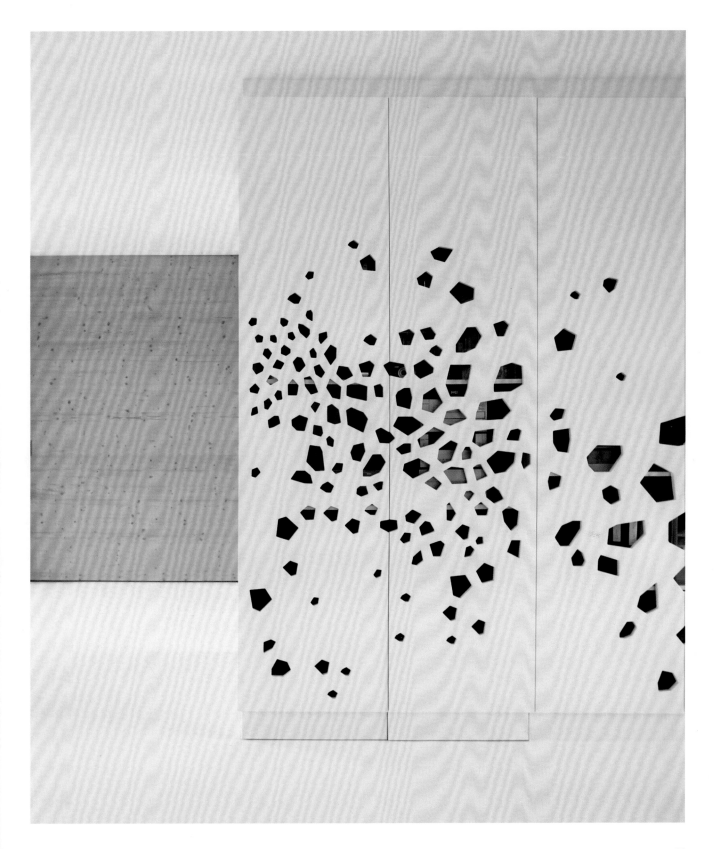

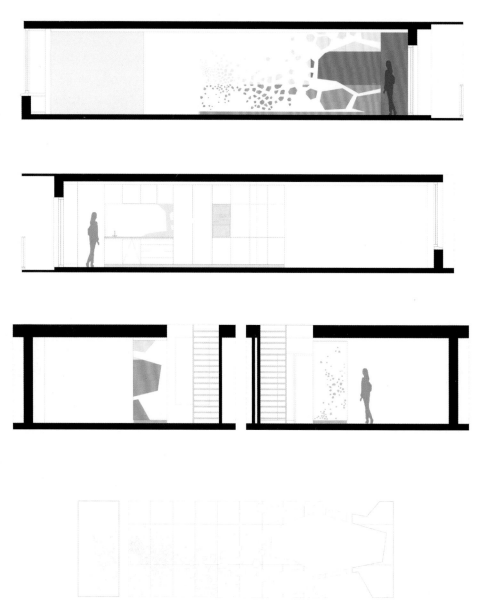

Kitchen sections

The holes are more than simply aesthetic, they also serve as handles for the cabinets. A shame they are also dust traps but that is one of the risks of originality.

Die Löcher sind mehr als nur eine ästhetische Spielerei: Es handelt sich um Griffe für die Kleiderschränke. Leider sind sie eben offen, so dass Staub eindringen kann. Das Risiko der Originalität.

Ces trous ne sont pas qu'esthétiques ; ce sont les poignées des armoires. Dommage qu'ils laissent aussi entrer la poussière. L'originalité a ses risques.

Los agujeros son más que una baza estética: son asideros para los armarios. Lástima que también sean un paso abierto para el polvo. Es el riesgo de lo original.

DUPLEX SANTA ENGRACIA

James & Mau
www.dethier.be
Liège, Belgium
1657 sq ft (154 m²)
© Serge Brison

This renovation project set out to combine two small duplexes into a single family home. The result gives the impression of having ripped a detached house from its plot on a modern urbanisation and stuffed it into a building in the middle of the city. The house was clad in wood and the terrace transformed into a garden. A house on top of a penthouse… sometimes things are just cool from the start.

Ein Einfamilienhaus, wie man sie oft in Wohnsiedlungen findet, wurde scheinbar aus dem Boden gerissen und in ein Gebäude inmitten der Stadt verpflanzt. Das war die Absicht hinter der Vereinigung der beiden kleinen Maisonnette-Wohnungen: die Errichtung eines *Hauses*. Hierfür musste die Terrasse als Garten herhalten, alles wurde mit Holz verkleidet. Ein Haus auf einem Dachboden: Manchmal ergeben sich einfach unvermeidbar schicke Ausgangspunkte.

Un logement familial que l'on trouve dans les lotissements, arraché au sol et posé dans un édifice au cœur de la ville. L'intention était de construire une *maison* en réunissant deux petits duplex. La terrasse a joué le rôle du jardin et le bois est l'unique revêtement. Une maison au-dessus des combles ; les débuts, parfois, sont tout simplement chics.

Una vivienda unifamiliar, de esas que uno halla en urbanizaciones, arrancada del suelo y metida en un edificio en medio de la ciudad. Esa fue la intención al remodelar esta unión de dos pequeños dúplex: construir una *casa*. Para ello, la terraza tuvo que hacer de jardín y la madera, que revestirlo todo. Una casa encima de un ático: a veces se dan puntos de partida irremediablemente chics.

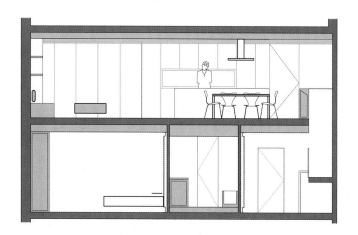

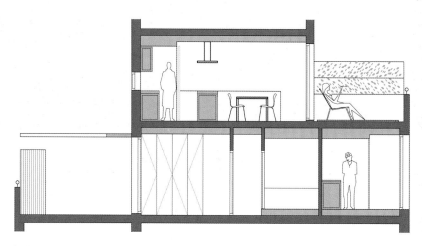

Longitudinal sections

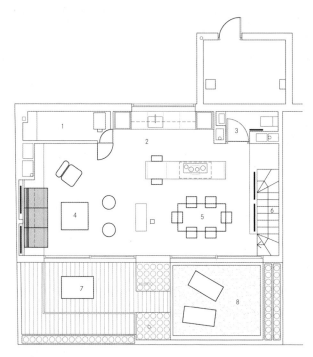

First floor plan

1. Storage room
2. Kitchen
3. Toilet
4. Hall
5. Dining room
6. Stairs
7. Terrace
8. Garden

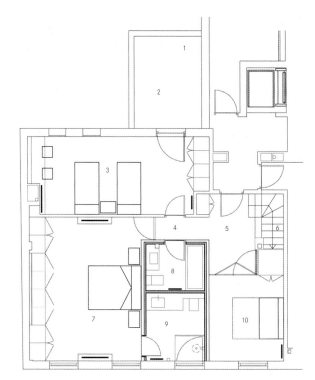

Ground floor plan

1. Sauna
2. Mini golf
3. Bedroom
4. Corridor
5. Entrance
6. Stairs
7. Master bedroom
8. Bathroom
9. Bathroom
10. Bedroom

The inspiration for the bathroom, say the architects, was "ice in a glass of whisky". This island of etched glass also separates the bedrooms.

Die Inspiration für das Badezimmer bestand laut dem Studio in dem „Eis in einem Whiskeyglas". Diese Insel aus Glas, die mit einem Siebdruck versehen wurde, trennt außerdem auch die Räume voneinander.

Selon l'agence, la salle de bains s'inspire d' « un glaçon dans un verre de whisky ». Cette île en verre sérigraphié sépare également les pièces.

La inspiración para el cuarto de baño, dicen desde el estudio, era el "hielo en un vaso de whisky". Esta isla de vidrio serigrafiado también separa las habitaciones.

VILLA PERINNE

JUMA architects
www.jumaarchitects.com
Duinbergen, Belgium
2126 sq ft (197,6 m^2)
© Liesbeth Goetschakckx

The biggest challenge in designing the interior of Villa Perinne was the fact that it was a new apartment in which the main body of the home and its finishes were already supplied. Although the work focused initially on improving the badly designed kitchen, bathroom and dressing room, in the end it took a complete renovation project to satisfy the desires of its owners.

Das größte Hindernis beim Design des Innenbereichs der Villa Perinne war das Arbeiten mit einer neuen Wohnung, deren vorhandene Form und Finish bleiben sollten. Ein Großteil der Aufmerksamkeit richtete sich auf die Verbesserung der Küche, des Bads und des Ankleidezimmers, die schlecht entworfen waren und für die schließlich eine vollständige Renovierung notwendig war, um den Wünschen der Besitzer gerecht zu werden.

Le principal inconvénient, lors de l'aménagement intérieur de la Villa Perinne, était d'intervenir dans un appartement neuf, aux murs et aux finitions existantes. Même si on s'est tout d'abord attaché à améliorer la cuisine, la salle de bains et le dressing, mal conçus, on a fini par une rénovation complète correspondant aux souhaits des propriétaires.

El hándicap principal en el diseño del interior de Villa Perinne era actuar sobre un apartamento nuevo, donde el cuerpo de la vivienda y los acabados venían dados. Pese a fijar en un principio la atención en la mejora de la cocina, el baño y el vestidor, mal diseñados, finalmente fue necesario un trabajo de renovación completo que satisficiera los deseos de los propietarios.

A large radiator dominated in the living room. This has been substituted with a unit that integrates the heat source without making it visible.

Im Wohnzimmer wurde ein großer Heizkörper, der die Aufmerksamkeit auf sich lenkte, durch ein Möbelstück ersetzt, in dem eine Wärmequelle eingebaut ist, die man einfach nicht sieht.

Dans le séjour, le grand radiateur qui attirait toute l'attention a été remplacé par un meuble qui incorpore la source de chaleur, en la rendant invisible.

En la sala de estar, un gran radiador que captaba toda la atención ha sido sustituido por un mueble que integra la fuente de calor sin que sea vista.